Make Your Backyard More Interesting Than TV

Jay Beckwith

Make Your Backyard More Interesting Than TV

Drawings by MICHAEL McMILLAN

McGraw-Hill Book Company

New York / St. Louis / San Francisco / Auckland / Bogotá / Düsseldorf
Johannesburg / London / Madrid / Mexico / Montreal / New Delhi / Panama
Paris / São Paulo / Singapore / Sydney / Tokyo / Toronto

Library of Congress Cataloging in Publication Data
Beckwith, Jay.
make your backyard more interesting than TV.
Bibliography: p.
1. Playgrounds—Apparatus and equipment. 2. Garden structures. 3. Family recreation. I. Title.
CV426.B42   790'.068   79-16093
ISBN 0-07-004266-7

First McGraw-Hill Paperback Edition

1 2 3 4 5 6 7 8 9 MUMU 8 7 6 5 4 3 2 1 0

Book design by Anita Walker Scott.

Warning to Manufacturers

The designs in this book are copyrighted and are intended strictly for the use of private individuals. Licenses to manufacture these designs can be obtained from the author. Modified designs more suitable for mass production and marketing assistance are also available. However, should an attempt be made to produce these designs without authorization, vigorous legal action will be taken.

Caution to Builders

The information on safety and designs contained in this book are the very best available to the author at the date of publication. Because each environment and each family is unique and the quality of construction will vary greatly, the author cannot be held responsible for injuries which result from the use of these designs.

The owner/builder is responsible for determining the appropriateness of the design to his or her needs, for the strength and integrity of the units, and for any modification required by the actual use patterns which emerge after installation. The author will be happy to provide advice to parents who are concerned with such matters, and may be contacted at 6753 Giovanetti Road, Forestville, California 95436.

Notice to Day Care Centers and Nursery Schools

The designs in this book are specially planned for backyard installation. Most are significantly better than anything else available for young children. They are not, however, designed for institutional use and cannot serve a large population. For instance, the decks are neither big enough nor connected in such a way as to accommodate the numbers of children generally present in day care settings. The materials are also under the scale and weight that would be required in an institutional setting.

If your program serves only a few children, and the play area is very similar to the normal backyard, you might be able to adapt some of the ideas in this book by taking special care to use heavyweight materials and enlarging the decks and attachments. These designs are inadequate for programs with more than half a dozen children and those with yards which could be used nights or weekends by children who climb over the fence.

For your own protection and long-term satisfaction, we strongly urge that your program use play equipment from commercial sources. (See Materials.) This equipment can be purchased in stages, installed by volunteers, easily maintained, and, above all, covered by insurance.

Published in association with **SAN FRANCISCO BOOK COMPANY.**

To HANNAH *who taught me parenthood and playfulness*

CONTENTS

PREFACE

The designs and information in this book are drawn from, and intended for, the real world. The units can be built with tools and materials available from neighborhood sources. The cost of the structures has been kept to an absolute minimum, yet with an emphasis on safe and sturdy construction. Some projects can be completed with just the cost of a trip to acquire various objects.

While exact plans are included for most of the designs, we hope that each family will modify the structures to make a play environment which meets their needs exactly. For that reason, enough information has been included to allow good decisions when adapting the units.

Although a well-designed play environment is one of the safest places for children, there are many things parents can do to minimize the potential for injury and, at the same time, maximize the developmental aspects of the play area. Thus, in addition to construction details, which are generally accepted as of low risk, we have included information on guiding children's use patterns.

Make Your Backyard More Interesting Than TV is a total resource for the creation of a developmentally sound and low-risk play environment which will enchant your children.

J.B.

Forestville, California
September 1979

I
Children and Play

Electronic Baby Sitters

Before TV, children spent much of their free time outdoors. They played games like hide-and-seek and Cowboys and Indians, built clubhouses and treehouses, and dug foxholes. Children always had marbles or jacks in their pockets, and they seemed to be in constant motion.

There has been a big change. Current research shows that many preschool children spend as much as one-third of their waking hours in front of "the tube." Many excellent books detail the effects of TV on children's lifestyle, thinking, and personality, allowing parents to take a critical look at the role of TV in their child's life.

Our purpose here is not to condemn television, but rather to offer parents simple, inexpensive, and effective alternatives. Television could not have penetrated so deeply into our homes if it had not filled an important need. The saying goes that TV is the nation's baby sitter. As with most sayings, it has more than a grain of truth.

While it may be distressing to think that our kids are absorbed for hours watching cartoon animals smash each other and are bombarded by the hard sell of white sugar, at the same time, we are glad to know that they are safe at home and not out on the streets. Even ten years ago, a parent could feel comfortable letting children play out-doors. The reality of life today is that, given traffic conditions and other dangers, we are reluctant to allow our children to explore their communities freely.

The neighborhood environment has not been the only change; our values have changed as well. Today, in many areas, single-parent families are the majority. Some schools report that as many as eighty-five per cent of our children are being raised by only one parent. This is a radical change in the fabric of American life. The spiraling rate of family dissolution is in itself an enormous problem, one that has not yet been addressed seriously by our national policy makers. It is also a symptom of even more profound changes.

Parents today feel that they must fulfill themselves as individuals. Raising a family is not enough for many parents; career, education, and personal growth are equally important. Many mothers are going back to school or joining the labor force, so even when the family stays together, both parents may be away from home a majority of the time.

After a hard day's work, it is easy to understand what a blessing that TV baby sitter can be. It gives parents time to prepare dinner, straighten up the house, and perhaps even relax a little.

Not only have our values and goals changed, the economic basis of our lives is also very different from what it once was. Today, we live in a period of material consumption previously unknown in human history. Our modern lifestyle brings greater demands and pressures with all the costly appliances that are supposed to save us labor, our great social mobility, and an incredible rate of inflation (especially in the cost of buying a home in a desirable neighborhood). Parents today must not only work very hard but also strive to advance as rapidly as possible in a very competitive environment. The specter of retirement without financial security is all too real and frightening.

It is clear that parents and families are under tremendous stress. We know that we ought to spend more time with our children, but time is money, and both are in short supply. So, to survive, we let our kids find their own amusements, and often they choose TV.

When Americans have a problem, they generally turn to the marketplace for a solution. Therefore, one of the first steps most parents take to create an alternative to TV is to look at the swing sets in the local department store.

A few parents will buy those candy-striped metal contraptions, but most will not. Most of us understand that equipment and a safe and interesting place to play are important for our children, and we know instinc-tively that those prefab gym sets miss the mark. If we are going to invest the time and money to create a good place to play, we should examine in depth the real function of play equipment.

A Playful Way to a Happy Home

When we create a play environment we hope our children will go outside and play quietly without supervision. Not only do parents want time that is free from the needs of children, the children also require time to work out their own interests without reliance on parents. A good outside play space, then, serves both the parent and the child, and, unlike television, can do so productively.

Inherent in play is the assumption that children are pursuing their own interests. Recent research has established that when children respond to their own needs and interests they build self-confidence and a positive image of themselves as competent individuals. It is the sense of "I can do it!" that fulfills a child and helps to develop a positive and effective personality.

In contrast, when children are required to live up to the expectations of others, when their lives are dominated by outside demands, they develop negative attitudes toward themselves and toward others. This does not mean that children should not have any responsibilities, but merely that they must also have time when they can "do their own thing." Free play is essential to a child's development.

Some play environments are more "child centered," that is, open to the child's spontaneous activity. These are called "creative play areas" because they allow children to follow their own interests. A play area with movable parts is more creative than one in which all the components are bolted down. A wide slide is more creative than a narrow slide because it allows more ways to move and play.

When the spaces we build for children are creative and child centered, the children can play there longer without supervision. There will be less need for adults to supply materials or guidance, and less aggressiveness between children.

Competition for limited play resources is one of the greatest causes of conflict between children. In an enriched environment there is much less of this competition. If the environment is also creative, adults will not be called in as referees nearly as often, and the conflicts that arise will be clearly personal and not built into the environment.

The play structures in this book are designed to maximize the amount of time children will play in and around them without adult involvement. They are as child centered and as open to the child's creativity as possible.

To create appropriate conditions that will maximize play opportunities, we should understand certain aspects of child development. The following section is not intended to describe the total development of your child, who is a unique and complex individual. Rather, we will look at general patterns of development as they relate to the design and creation of play environments that make our backyards more interesting than TV.

Rough-and-Tumble Growing Up

Motor activity is the most visible part of play, with running, swinging, and climbing frequent elements. The child's body is programmed by nature to seek a high level of rough-and-tumble activity which promotes development in many ways.

Development of coordination is one function of hard, physical play. The simple act of standing up and walking is composed of hundreds of discrete motor components which begin when the infant first raises his head.

Each of these steps has an instinctive, or reflex, component which nature has preprogrammed into the child's brain. No one teaches a child to walk; it is an innate ability. Through play, these separate actions are coordinated into behavior that does not require conscious control.

Hard, physical play is nature's way of bodybuilding. Through motor play the child acquires basic movement skills which are practiced until they are coordinated and so well learned that the child performs them automatically.

A good analogy is that the child is like a student driver. At first it requires complete attention just to steer the car and to remember the shift and clutch patterns. Later these things come naturally, and the driver can carry on other activities with complete confidence, like talking while driving. In fact, if we did not learn to use our bodies automatically, we would be in real danger if we had to stop and think things out before reacting.

Some children do not have natural automatic control of all their motor or posture systems. Children who must use part of their attention to consciously control their bodies are often identified by poor academic performance. They are unable to follow classroom activities because of "cognitive overload"—like the new driver who is so intent on keeping the car under control that, when suddenly asked to turn left, he forgets which direction to go.

A child learns very long sequences of movements. Walking, bicycling, and swimming, for example, all combine many smaller skills. Play is perfectly suited for teaching these activities and for the integration of highly complex motor sequences. It is a particularly effective strategy to teach motor skills because it requires no cognitive thought.

In a way, play is mindless. It is this quality of not really thinking about moving that seems to promote motor learning. While children are aware only that they are playing Cowboys and Indians, the intellectual centers of their brains are occupied with conversation, imagination, and game strategies, and their bodies are working on improving performance. We adults might take a lesson from children when learning a motor skill: it may be best not to concentrate but rather to play.

There is considerable current research on the developmental sequence of motor reflexes and the kinds of learning disorders that may result when this sequence is disrupted. It is fairly well established that many learning and behavior dysfunctions are caused by a motor and/or reflex deficiency. This research emphasizes that the healthy, normal child must be permitted to follow nature's plan for the body's growth and development.

The understanding that there is a natural evolution of physical skill, and that this progression is innate, does not mean that the child is a biological robot. Just watching the pure joy of the infant who is learning to walk will convince anyone that gaining mastery over the body is a highly rewarding and enjoyable experience. Unlike we adults who improve our physical condition only with some difficulty (and often with some pain), children seem unperturbed by hard falls or hours of intense activity.

Those who try to protect children from risks by limiting their access to challenges

only postpone necessary learning encounters to a time when their bodies will not be as flexible nor reach their limits as comfortably. It is better to allow your children to take chances and progress at their own pace than to overprotect them in the mistaken belief that they will be better able to handle risks when they are older.

Most parents recognize intuitively the importance of active play for their children. The word "play" immediately conjures thoughts of swings and slides. In fact, traditional playground equipment does provide some good motor experience. This equipment has been popular since the coming of the industrial revolution and has survived unchanged for more than a hundred years.

The standard playground contains swings, slides, merry-go-rounds, climbers, and teeter-totters. These units are made small for young children and progressively larger for older children. If we use the same kinds of traditional designs for a backyard setting, we, too, will encounter this size problem. As our children get bigger, the equipment also must grow in size. But what if we have several children over a wide age span? Do we have to change the equipment constantly or, for example, have several swings of different sizes?

Although there are easy solutions to this problem, it is clear that the department store swing sets do not provide play experiences suitable for all ages. In fact, this equipment has been designed only for the age range from four to six years.

Traditional play equipment, whether in a park or from the department store, has another shortcoming in addition to size. Equipment that provides essentially the same challenges for all ages completely ignores an important fact: children are not only getting bigger, they are also learning.

A two-year-old will use the traditional slide as the manufacturer intended, carefully climbing the ladder, sitting at the top and sliding down in a seated position. A three-year-old will go down the slide in any position imaginable. A four-year-old will run up the slide, and a five-year-old will jump from the top. By six, the child may ignore the slide entirely, having explored every conceivable physical challenge the equipment offers. Although most of this exploration would be considered "misuse—not intended by the manufacturer," it is the child's natural search for challenging motor play which leads to this "misuse" and often to injury.

It is not children who are to blame if they are hurt trying to extract a meaningful physical experience from a piece of play equipment. We adults should know that children develop increased ability and seek new challenges. Therefore, correctly designed play equipment must allow children the utmost

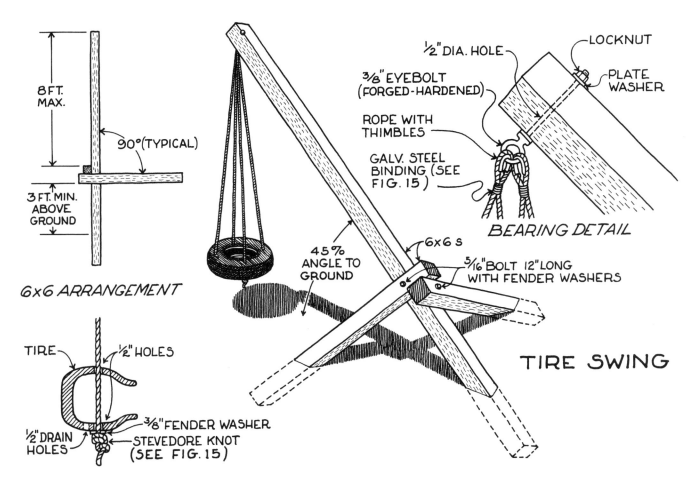

8FT. MAX.

90°(TYPICAL)

3 FT. MIN. ABOVE GROUND

6×6 ARRANGEMENT

TIRE

½" HOLES

½" DRAIN HOLES

⅜" FENDER WASHER

STEVEDORE KNOT (SEE FIG. 15)

½" DIA. HOLE

⅜" EYEBOLT (FORGED-HARDENED)

ROPE WITH THIMBLES

GALV. STEEL BINDING (SEE FIG. 15)

LOCKNUT

PLATE WASHER

BEARING DETAIL

45% ANGLE TO GROUND

6×6 s

5/16" BOLT 12" LONG WITH FENDER WASHERS

TIRE SWING

Figure 1

exploration of their physical abilities in an acceptably safe manner.

We know that the backyard play area requires equipment that is flexible enough to accommodate children of various sizes (or one growing child). We also know that play equipment must be designed to challenge children at various stages of development. These two factors are very important to the correct design of play environments. They require equipment which can be easily modified for both size and function and which can be played on safely in many ways.

There is one more important design consideration for active play equipment: space. A single swing, for example, requires an open area of ten by eighteen feet. Any equipment which can be climbed should be set back from an obstruction by a distance equal to its height. By this standard, a small climber four feet square and eight feet high requires 400 square feet; that is, eight feet of setback each side of the four-foot structure for a total of twenty feet on a side.

As subsequent sections of this book will show, we can do many things to provide active play which is both challenging and efficient. However, unless you are prepared to undertake the construction of a complete recreational facility, your backyard play environment will not meet all of your children's physical play needs.

The neighborhood park, a well-designed school playground, nature experiences, and good physical education are all essential to your child's complete physical development. The backyard play structure will complement, but not totally replace, these experiences in the world outside the home.

A Balancing Act

One might think that balance would be a motor activity. However, while there are motor aspects to balancing skills, they are only the result of a more basic system which is fundamentally perceptual. It is important to discuss these two systems separately to fully understand how they work together.

The balance system is perhaps more critical to humans than to any other animal. Walking erect, with the complete torso balanced over the pelvis, requires a very high degree of skill. Even slight disturbances in the balance system can create major posture problems, leg deformities, or foot abnormalities.

The major perceptual organs of this system are found in the inner ear. There is also a strong neurological connection between the inner ear and the eyes because, in addition to its role in posture, the inner ear plays a critical role in the perception of motion. We experience many kinds of motion simul-

taneously: objects in the environment, the whole person, the head in relation to the body, and the eye in relation to the head may all be moving at once. The ability to distinguish and comprehend these relative motions is very difficult, yet we perform it routinely and with great accuracy.

When sitting at a stoplight, you might think your car is rolling. You suddenly apply the brakes, only to discover that it was the car next to yours that was moving. This is one of the few times you can be fooled by the balance system because the motion was so slow that it was below the perceptual threshold.

It is important to note that the balance system is better at detecting acceleration than speed. In terms of the play area, this means that children are actually more interested in starting and stopping quickly than in going fast; acceleration and deceleration are more exciting than speed.

Balance play, like motor play, has an innate biological motivation. Children seek out experiences which stimulate the balance system, such as running, jumping, spinning, and swinging. Children pursue even higher levels of stimulation by hanging upside down or closing their eyes while in motion. All healthy children do this to some extent and it is a normal activity.

As the balance system is excited, the areas of the brain responsible for processing balance information become increasingly specialized to handle the job more efficiently. When this process is completed, the child no longer feels as strong an urge to behave in a way that excites the balance system.

We can now understand from this study of the balance system why children enjoy rapid acceleration, will often hang upside down, and in general seek to stimulate the inner ear. One of the best means of providing for this need is a tire swing (*Figure 1*). This swing allows to-and-fro motion, and can also be spun at a very satisfying speed. We should also provide children with equipment such as turning bars from which they can hang.

"I'm Batman, You're Robin"

Until they are about one and a half years old, children are simply unable to cooperate or communicate in a manner that allows them to play together. At this stage, play is very difficult to distinguish from exploration as children are absorbed in pulling, grabbing, and mostly putting into their mouths anything they find in their environment. For this reason, we must take special care to remove small or toxic items from the child's environment. Children may even swallow quantities of sand, so it is probably a good

idea not to leave them outdoors unattended.

From the age of one and a half to two and a half, children can play in the same space with other children in relative peace. This is not genuine social play in a technical sense; if you watch closely you will notice that the children do not interact but are simply doing the same things. This parallel play should be monitored closely by parents since it is a delicate balance likely to result in pushes and tears.

From age two and a half on up, children begin to cooperate. This marks the beginning of true social play. The first few years of this process are particularly important, and there is much parents can do to help their children maximize their growth potential at this stage. Obviously, if a child is to learn to interact, he will need to be with other children. This socialization process is one of the most important functions of a good day care center. Neighborhood children of siblings can also fill the need for social interaction with peers.

Through social play the child learns to be a winner or a loser in life. The process of being accepted and having friends can be very risky. In play, when a child says, "I'm Batman and you're Robin," he is taking a leadership role and trying to get his playmate to take a subservient role. If his friend says, "Nah, let's play Battle Star, and I'll be

Captain," then the play structure initially proposed has been rejected. This failure is painful. On the other hand, the child's playmate may say, "Yeah! You play Batman, and I'll be Superman." Thus the child's plan for play is accepted, but his friend chooses to relate as an equal. This is the kind of strategic maneuvering which characterizes much of social play and makes it such a powerful influence on a child's self-concept.

The role of fantasy is important when trying to understand both the child's social play, and, as we will see in the next section, his constructive play. The fantasy element in play is the child's attempt to fabricate reality through imagination. Acting out the imagined situation is not essential to fantasy play, but the combination of imagination and motor activity seems to be profoundly related.

A recent study showed that children who engaged in fantasy play in an active, physical way had a measurable I.Q. increase over children who were passive. In the test, three groups of children were exposed to different situations. One group acted out fantasy stories, one acted out real-life situations, and the third group listened to fairy stories.

Both of the active groups not only showed the I.Q. increase but also demonstrated significantly better behavior control. It was suggested that these children learned to use their imagination to keep them entertained in a boring situation and that this accounted for their superior control over impulsive behavior. If the action aspect of play is so important to full development of the child's intellect and behavior, we may indeed be damaging children by replacing normal, active fantasy play with passive TV watching.

To promote active social play we cannot simply put children together and expect them to get along well. Their interaction will tend to become more positive as the environment is enriched. In a complex space, children have more to focus on outside themselves, and more objects allow spontaneous games and imagination to move from one situation to another.

If there is one message that this book seeks to convey, it is that children play best in a complex environment. This should seem obvious, but the world we adults create for children is often just the opposite. A standard swing set, for example, is designed for individual experiences in a sterile environment. Even many well-intentioned parents create spaces which may please the adult sense of order but which are devoid of any real opportunities for children to play.

Kids Build Their Own Worlds

The enrichment of space is not only crucial to active physical and social play, it is also essential to constructive play. When children build cities with blocks, draw freeways in the dirt for their "hot wheels," or set up doll houses, they are engaging in constructive play.

Fantasy and make-believe should be considered an essential part of constructive play when designing play areas. It is imagination which allows children to overcome the deficiencies in their environment by pretending that they are driving a car or flying a spaceship. Thus, contrary to common belief, fantasy play is not an escape from reality, but rather an attempt to approximate it more closely.

Clearly, children can do amazing things with imagination. Once we understand that this fantasizing is a compensation for the lack of detail in the environment, it becomes clear why a rich environment is more supportive of play than a sterile one. If a play environment consists only of swings and a slide, it will fail to provide for constructive play. On the other hand, by adding such loose parts as walking boards, ropes, buckets, ladders, and pieces of canvas, we can make constructive play a constant and important part of the children's activity.

Unlike social play, constructive play can occur when your child plays alone and is, in fact, the dominant type of play with solitary children. Constructive play is one of the most important means by which children investigate their environment. They are using tools—whether they be hammers or words and images—and through this play, increase their capacity to manipulate them. Thus, constructive play is the forerunner of later intellectual skills. One of the best investments a parent can make in building a child's intellectual and tool-using capabilities is to provide a rich environment that supports constructive play.

Safety, Liability, and Mother Nature

To achieve a hassle-free environment in which children can play for long periods without supervision, we need to examine in detail the issue of safety. Of course, it would be ideal for no accident to ever occur. Obviously, that is impossible, as safety is relative.

The most constructive way to approach safety is not to attempt to prevent all accidents, but rather to reduce to an acceptable level the chance of occurrence. Should the outside play area be as safe for the child as being indoors? Should it be safer than riding in a car? Most parents are willing to allow the outside play area to be more risky than the indoors, but hope it is safer than the family car!

In the preceding pages, we have gained an understanding of the basic needs of children, and thus have already acquired the most important tools for creating a safe play environment. A child-centered play area is much safer than traditional play situations. (I said earlier that child centered means a place for spontaneous activity; another meaning is that the environment is fitted to the children, rather than trying to fit the children to the environment.)

For example, we have seen that children seek motor activity, social interaction, and acceleration. From this we can predict the typical use pattern of play equipment like swings. The child's first interest is in the hypnotic pendulum motion of swinging back and forth. Soon the child will be trying to pump the swing herself. This is an important accomplishment, for when the child can pump the swing she is no longer considered a baby. Once the skill of swinging is mastered, though, where is the next challenge?

In order to intensify the experience, children will pump the swing higher and higher, until they finally get a free-fall jolt at the top of the arc. Next, they will try jumping out of the swing, and it will become a contest to see how far out they can fly. If they want to add a social play component, about the only

thing they can do—beyond pushing each other, is to try to bump into or wrap their legs around each other.

While some of these swing activities are safe, others are quite dangerous. We all did these things on swings when we were kids and yet we think our children will not. We can preserve most of the good aspects of the traditional swing experience by substituting a tire swing. It is even possible to "pump" a tire swing and to add new activities like spinning and group play. In this way, we enhance the swinging experience and, at the same time, eliminate most of the hazards.

Besides making our play equipment more child centered, there are several other things we can do to improve the safety of the play environment. Three-quarters of all playground injuries result from falls from equipment. The dangerous aspects of falls can be reduced by using soft ground cover and removing hazards in potential fall zones.

However, we cannot eliminate all danger, nor should we want to. Children will take risks and will climb anywhere they think they can go, constantly attempting to extend their ability and challenge themselves. Knowing this, we should be prepared for children to try everything they can imagine, and realize that a fall might occur since they are at the limits of their ability.

Falling on something hard or sharp naturally hurts more than falling on something

Figure 2

soft. You should therefore create a fall zone free of obstacles around any structure which children might climb.

A fall zone of fifteen feet covered with foam rubber might be ideal for safety, but it is totally impractical. To be effective, you must maintain an area of at least five feet, free of all obstructions, around all play equipment. This is an *absolute* minimum. If the area is smaller, your children *will* fall on whatever is within that zone.

To provide greater safety, the fall zone should be made proportionately larger for taller structures. Therefore, a structure with the highest point of eight feet should have a fall zone of eight feet. If this standard is observed, your child will be protected from all but the most extraordinary situations or will have to purposely jump beyond the fall zone. Hopefully, we are creating a play area interesting enough that children will not seek this kind of challenge.

The fall zone should be free of obstructions and should also be covered with fall-absorbing material. The best ground cover is round particle sand. Sand has been proven to absorb falls better than most other materials and is itself a great play material, enhancing the play value of the space. In the first part of the design section, we will examine in detail the use of sand and discuss its sanitation and other related issues.

Pea gravel is nearly as safe as round particle sand. The roundness of the sand or gravel is important because crushed rock sand or angular particle gravel packs very densely and loses most of its value as a cushion. The sand or pea gravel should be clean and free of fine dust or clay, as these particles will create a cleanliness problem and also contribute to the compacting of the ground cover by filling in the small spaces between the larger particles. The only thing that makes pea gravel somewhat less safe than sand is that, when thrown, it may cause more eye injury than sand.

There is a material available in some areas called "birds-eye gravel" or "grain" which is a texture between pea gravel and sand. It is often sold for aquarium bottoms and is sometimes not available in large quantities. The diameter of the particles is less than one-fourth and larger than one-eighth inch.

One of the most desirable qualities of sand or gravel is that it drains very well. When installed to the recommended depth of eight inches, it will withstand quite a heavy rain and still be playable very soon after the rain stops.

Various kinds of tree products—tanbark, fir bark, wood chips, and sawdust—are all good cushions for the fall zone. The major drawback of these materials is that they eventually decompose and must be replaced. Also, they are often dirtier than sand or gravel because of the dust created as they are ground down under the children's feet. They also drain very poorly. The main advantage of these materials is that they tend not to be tracked indoors as much as sand and, once inside, they are easier to clean up and less destructive to floors and rugs.

There are commercial playground rubber mats available which are the cleanest ground cover of all. These mats are very expensive, approximately three dollars per square foot, and must be applied over asphalt or concrete. During a preliminary investigation sponsored by the U.S. Consumer Product Safety Commission, rubber matting did not meet the suggested standards for preventing injuries.

Soil is not an effective fall cushion since it compacts readily and becomes nearly as hard as concrete. When wet, soil turns to mud and makes the play area useless. Grass also is ineffective since foot traffic kills it and exposes the underlying dirt. Astroturf has insufficient padding; straw or leaves decompose even faster than wood chips. Your final selection between organic or inorganic material will be based on availability, cost, and personal preference. In general, however, the child-centered play area will use sand as ground cover.

In addition to maintaining a clear fall zone with a soft landing surface, you can reduce injuries from falls by keeping the heights of structures to a minimum. The designs presented in this book have the highest deck at six feet. This is high enough for a reasonably interesting slide and also to make a play space underneath the deck. If the safety rail is three feet above the deck, then the highest point would be nine feet, still an acceptable distance when falling onto a good ground cover.

Our adult tendency is to try to make a structure more interesting by making it taller. It is true that great height is more frightening, but is it more challenging? The same risks can be taken at a lower level and, if the child should fall, the consequences are not so dear. Knowing this, children will actually take more risks on a low structure and still be safer than on a high one. Therefore, a low structure can be both more challenging *and* safer. The low structure also can be used over a longer period of time since the very young can use it with caution and the older child can use it with abandon.

Besides being creative, low and set in sand, the play structure should also be free of sharp edges or places that can entrap children. Children should not be allowed to play on any climbable structure when wearing loose clothing. Coats with hoods or ponchos are particularly dangerous. Capes should be made of paper or easily break away. Costumes like fancy dresses and high-heeled shoes that are used in fantasy play must not be allowed on climbing structures.

Children should also be taught to be cautious when carrying objects. While it might be best not to allow kids to carry anything while playing, this would be impossible and impractical. Therefore, we must teach them to be careful with such objects.

When selecting sand toys, fantasy play props, or other loose parts, remember that these will be carried throughout the play environment and evaluate them for potential hazards. Often substitutions can be made: rubber swords and plastic unbreakable shovels are available. Some toys may look safe but, when broken, present sharp edges. You should watch for these as part of the regular inspection of the play area.

Some tools are important in constructive play but are also potentially hazardous. For example, a screwdriver is an important tool for constructive activities. The children must learn to recognize the danger inherent in the tool, to keep the tool in its proper place, and to use it only for its intended purpose. If they are not mature enough to learn to respect the hazards presented by such objects, then they must not be permitted to play with them.

The play structures must be built with quality materials in a craftsmanlike manner and must be inspected regularly. Pay particular attention to swing bearings, ladder rungs, and edges of the slide, and to the proper distribution of ground cover. In older structures, periodic checks for rotted wood are also necessary.

Even if you take all precautions, there may be an injury. There are two things which you can do to minimize the consequences of these accidents. First, develop a family emergency plan. A good book on first aid for children is *Sigh of Relief* (*see Bibliography*). Second, neighborhood children should not be allowed to play in your backyard unless you have had contact with their parents. Ideally, they should come and see the play area and discuss what procedure to follow if an emergency should develop. By establishing a foundation of understanding and communication, you can reduce the possibility of unpleasant and costly complications.

The child and his parents should be made aware of the rules for using the equipment. These arrangements are only sensible and should be standard practice between parents even when a play structure is not being developed. When you create an interesting place to play, children probably will choose to play there instead of at someone else's house or out on the street. This increased use of your home will, in turn, increase your exposure to problems. You should have a homeowner's insurance policy that adequately protects you from liability claims.

Closely related to the question of safety is the use of play equipment in bad weather. There are some conditions under which children should not play on equipment. Slippery steel rungs and frozen sand are real hazards. However, most parents tend to be overprotective. Bad weather does create worry about colds, and nobody wants to clean up after messy children. On the other hand, the seasons and bad weather are a part of life, and children should experience them directly with all their senses. Properly attired and cautioned about ice, children can play outdoors safely in surprisingly bad weather and still enjoy themselves.

Building Codes

Municipal building codes have two functions. One is to make sure that structures are built in a durable and aesthetic manner. The other is to be certain that the assessed value of property is accurate for tax collection.

While building codes are not intended to apply to play structures, there are two situations which could involve you with the building assessor. If your community has a nit-picking assessor's office, they will make you get a permit to put up a mail box. Or, your structure may really offend one of your neighbors if, for example, it is placed right next to a fence that overlooks their pool and destroys their privacy.

Before you run down to City Hall, ask a few local contractors if they think a permit would be required in your neighborhood. If the building inspector is unavoidable, there are two routes open: you can get a permit or make your structure portable. (Building permits are almost never required for portable play equipment.) The designs in this book will satisfy any but the most stringent building codes. If you prepare an accurate and detailed drawing of your unit, it should be enough to secure approval.

Most of the designs presented here can be made portable. Portability makes the units more difficult to build and limits some design options but has the advantage of easy relocation.

If your play structure is modest in size, and you are considerate of your neighbors, you really need not be concerned with securing a building permit.

Summary

Parents who have found television essential as a baby sitter are now beginning to question its effects. Concerned parents are looking for ways to provide more active experiences for their children. While there are commercial play structures available, these are inadequate.

To interest children, a good play environment must meet their natural needs for play. These can be simplified into four basic categories: motor, balance, social, and constructive.

Motor play is very active. It is the primary way the child learns coordination and movement skills.

Balance play involves the inner ear and vision system. It develops reflexes and the ability to comprehend the relative movement of objects in the environment.

Social play involves the child's activity with others and the development of communication skills. Through social play children learn role models and develop language ability.

Constructive play is a physical or cognitive activity involving the skill of manipulating words, tools, and objects. It may be a quiet, solitary activity or a group project.

A safe play structure will be low and placed over a soft, fall-absorbing material. It should offer many activities to maintain the child's interest over a long period of time. A creative or child-centered environment is thus designed to meet most of the child's four basic play needs and allows him to explore his potential to the fullest.

Because children seek excitement and challenge as they learn and develop their abilities, they may be injured when they overextend themselves. While most dangers can be eliminated, no life experience is hazard-free, so each family should have a plan of action for emergencies. Also, because a child's play is social and involves other children, it is important that his playmates' parents be informed of the potential for injury and that they inspect the play environment.

II
Child Development

Each Child Is Unique

Every child is special and develops at an individual pace. More often than not, however, parents make the mistake of expecting too much too soon from their children. Instead of enjoying and celebrating our children's achievements at whatever age they occur, we try to make them fit into some hypothetical "normal" pattern. For that reason, a list of stages of development can be more of a hindrance than a help.

On the other hand, a child will be screened when he enters public school or first attends nursery school. So, whether we like it or not, standards will be applied to measure our child's maturity.

These screenings are intended to identify those children who have a developmental problem which may prevent them from achieving their full potential. In the last ten years, enormous strides have been made in remedying these problems. The stigma which was once applied to such children disappeared following the discovery that twenty per cent of all children have some form of specific developmental delay, and that every child can benefit from the activities which were once thought to be purely remedial. This realization was first established with the work of Maria Montessori, who developed her ideas while teaching retarded children.

The following list of developmental stages must be taken only as very general guidelines. The stages and examples used have been selected from several screening tests and remedial programs.

For instance, children tested when entering public school will be asked to jump over an object. If they do not lead with one foot, the tester will know that they have not established a dominant side. This, in turn, suggests that certain tasks, such as reading, _may_ be more difficult. The solution to this problem is _not_ training the child to jump with one foot forward. If parents try to train their kids to pass these tests it will only mask any underlying problems and prevent their detection and remedy.

When using the guidelines, if you should notice that your child is significantly behind his age group in achieving a certain skill, you should learn more about the relationship between physical development and learning. The Bibliography lists several good sources that will give you basic information on this area. You should also discuss your concern with teachers or diagnosticians, because early detection of these problems makes corrective measures much faster and simpler. It would be unwise to attempt your own therapeutic program without professional guidance.

DEVELOPMENTAL PHASES

12 to 24 Months: Walking and Talking

This is the age at which a child masters the art of walking. Initially, just standing unassisted and making some forward progress is all that he can manage. But very soon walking becomes easy and the child can stop and start without falling down. Near the end of this period, many children will be able to run awkwardly and walk a few steps backwards and sideways.

While this process progresses children also learn to thrust their arms forward when falling. This is called the protective arm reflex. You should notice if it is an automatic response; if it is not, you should provide remedial sensory motor activities. (*See Bibliography.*)

Balance is one of the key ingredients for successful walking. The balance system develops sufficiently during this period so that the child can jump in place or stand on one foot and kick a large ball. Coordination also improves and the child will be able to imitate clapping. Stacking blocks four to six high to build towers is a favorite activity, as is filling and dumping containers. At this age, the sandbox with blocks and empty cans is the center of the child's play world.

25 to 36 Months: "No!" and "Why?"

By this age mobility has increased greatly. The child can walk on tiptoe, go downstairs holding the railing, or go upstairs alternately leading with the left and right feet. This characteristic of leading with one foot will also show up during jumps or when standing on one foot. Tricycle riding is usually mastered by the age of three. Children will also be able to catch a large ball rolled to them.

This is the age at which role playing commences and hats, pots and pans, and other role-playing props will be rapidly put to use. In some respects, this is the most difficult age period for parents. The child has discovered "No!" and uses it incessantly. Together with the never-ending questions, "What's that?" and "Why?" it can make this age a trial.

The delightful aspect of toddlers is the curiosity and wonder they bring to every experience. Seeing the tiniest detail in their picture books or discovering that five rings of different sizes can be stacked up to make a tower really thrills them.

37 to 48 Months: "Let's Be Friends"

This is the age during which play apparatus really becomes the focus of children's play activity. They master climbing ladders, and going down the slide becomes routine. Just being pushed in the swing is not enough: "I wanna pump myself!" Twirling and spinning in the tire swing is also very popular and is an important activity for developing equilibrium.

A low turning bar should be available in the play area because, at this age, the horizontal midline of the body is being established. You will often see children leaning over the bar or wearing excessively tight belts.

Use of the thumb and middle or index finger to grasp objects develops during this age. Smaller objects can now be used constructively in the sand play area. The child should have mastered both body awareness and space. Thus, the concepts of going in and out, going up and down, being next to or away from, will become easy for the child to understand.

This is also the age during which true cooperative play with other children emerges. It is now possible for the child to take turns and share toys. Games with characters are acted out almost constantly.

4 to 5½ Years: Independence

This is the age when the child emerges as an independent person. For the first time he will start visiting neighborhood friends on his own. Parents are generally comfortable with this independence because the child is also willing to accept limits. The nature of the child's play is transformed and the first games with rules are made up and played spontaneously.

Locomotor skills have been mastered by this period. The child can gallop, make quick stops or turns on request, and skip and hop with ease. An obstacle course is fun at this age and the child can manage a four-inch balance beam and jump over six-inch objects.

The limited role playing of the three-year-old blossoms into real, constructive play. Structures of various sizes are built with blocks and other shapes. The child can carry around fairly heavy objects, up to twelve pounds, so building activities take on a new dimension. Hand-eye coordination has improved to the extent that the child can pour from containers into cups, dribble a ball, or bat a balloon in the air for a minute.

The platforms on the play structure become a focus for all sorts of elaborate games. With the child's new ability to play with neighborhood friends, the backyard will now be very busy and noisy.

5½ to 7 Years: Time of Testing

Up to this age a child's body has acted as a unit. Now he is able to use his right and left sides independently. For example, during play on the horizontal ladder, children will initially only be able to support their weight. Then they will be able to move from rung to rung, leading with the same dominant hand, and finally, swing freely leading with both hands alternately.

Dexterity and balance are so good by this time that children can oppose all fingers to the thumb or balance on one foot with their eyes closed. In fact, they may be able to do both at the same time, for they are now able to do two motor tasks simultaneously. They can rotate a foot at the ankle or a hand at the wrist without moving other body parts. They can use a hammer with only one hand.

This is the age of testing during which the child develops the sense of self-competence and self-confidence. A typical phrase is, "I can do that myself!" Well, sometimes they can and sometimes they can't, but in any case, they have to try. A lot of this testing occurs during play. Children of this age are often overheard saying "I'll bet you can't!" Because of this tendency to test their abilities to the limits, parents should keep a watchful eye on their children's play patterns and set up rules so that they do not get into activities that are obviously dangerous.

7 Years and Up: Years of Strength

By the seventh year, most of the various fundamental motor patterns have been established. Children can perform basic skills, like hand-over-hand motion on the horizontal ladder or a "sloth hang" from the bars.

Further development will now be along two dimensions: coordinating two or more tasks and increasing strength and endurance. This is the age at which the child can begin to perform sequential tasks, like the hop-skip-and-jump. Before this age the child could not keep three tasks in mind long enough to perform such a series of actions.

To challenge children at this age, the adult can make suggestions like, "Try to do that backwards. Now, try it backwards with your eyes closed." The idea is to handicap the child so that the basic skills are made more difficult. Stringing several tasks together will also make the activities more demanding and interesting.

After the eighth year, children become increasingly interested in the real world. They are not content with merely doing pull-ups; they want to know what the Guinness record is for consecutive pull-ups. Kids begin comparing their performance with their friends and their own past achievements. This is the age when the free play of childhood grows into a lifelong interest in physical fitness and participation in sports.

III
Play
Components

PLAY EQUIPMENT AND ITS USES

The purpose of *Make Your Backyard More Interesting Than TV* is not to provide parents with a physical education program for their children. Rather, the emphasis is on creating a rich and complex environment that supports the child's natural development and on introducing valuable activities for children that allow parents more productive time for their own needs.

The suggestions for activities on the various pieces of play equipment have been kept to a minimum. Parents who would like additional ideas should consult the books listed in the Bibliography.

We highly recommend that *every* parent read the suggestions for using the equipment, even though you may have no intention of teaching movement skills. Such a reading will acquaint the future builder of play structures with the functions of all the attachments. This will allow a much more educated selection of play features and will reduce the temptation to just build a swing and slide set.

The patterns of activities listed in this section are not only ones which may be taught; they are also the patterns which are likely to be naturally manifested by the children. Therefore, by reading this material, you will generally be able to anticipate the kinds of activities each piece of equipment will tend to stimulate.

The information on usage is intended to increase the challenge of the environment while reducing the level of hazard. Using ideas like, "do it backwards," or "do it with your eyes closed," the children are able to exact a higher level of challenge from equipment that they otherwise would have completely mastered.

Parents should take a few hours a month to introduce some of these skills. In this way, they can not only evaluate the child's progress and overall development, but also will be able to act as spotters during the child's first experiences with the more difficult tasks.

Whether you follow such a program or not, it is absolutely essential that your children ask permission before trying a new and challenging motor activity on the play structure. They should not try a new "trick" without your acting as a safety spotter. This is even more true of neighborhood children. If the kids start a game of gymnastics, they should let you know so that you can monitor their activities.

Swings

Swinging begins as a passive activity; the children are pushed in the swing. At this stage, the swing seat ought to hold the child securely so that there is no chance of his falling out. This will let you step away from the swing while the child coasts.

At about three years of age children can

begin to learn to pump a swing. Most children learn this skill only by watching other children and imitating their behavior.

While the child is learning to pump there is a golden opportunity to teach a fundamental principle of mechanics: why does pumping make a swing go? The effect of pumping can be demonstrated by setting up a pendulum. Take an object that weighs about a pound, connect a four-foot piece of string and hang it from a convenient place. Set the pendulum in motion, then have your child place an obstacle (like a pencil) in the path of the string, about a foot above the weight and directly under the support. Ask the child to describe what happens. After the pencil contacts the string, the weight moves faster because the pendulum has been shortened.

This experiment makes it relatively easy for a child to understand how pulling back on the swing chains and pulling up his legs makes the swing go faster and higher. The child should now be able to explain how you can pump standing in the seat.

A child can increase the sensation of movement by lying back in the swing and looking up at the sky. This effect is made even stronger when children close their eyes. The to-and-fro swing will later have to be replaced with a tire swing which allows spinning and group play.

Slides

STANDARD SLIDES

These are appropriate for relatively young children. They are a big challenge for the two and a half year old who must be assisted and monitored while sliding. By three and a half the child will be able to use the slide independently and will begin to experiment. Sliding headfirst and upside down are the next activities, and an adult should act as a spotter at the bottom of the slide for the first few attempts. Around four and a half the platform at the top of the slide becomes the focal point for dramatic play. At this point, the slide is more often used as an entrance, by running up it, than as an exit.

BANISTER SLIDES

Two or more inclined pipes can also be made into a slide. Besides being much easier and cheaper to build, these slides are much more challenging and creative. The very young child will not be able to use a banister slide, but after the age of three, children develop increasingly complex ways of going both up and down the banister slide. You can be certain children have learned to coordinate both sides of their bodies if they can go up the banister, because one hand must grip while the opposite arm reaches out to pull upward.

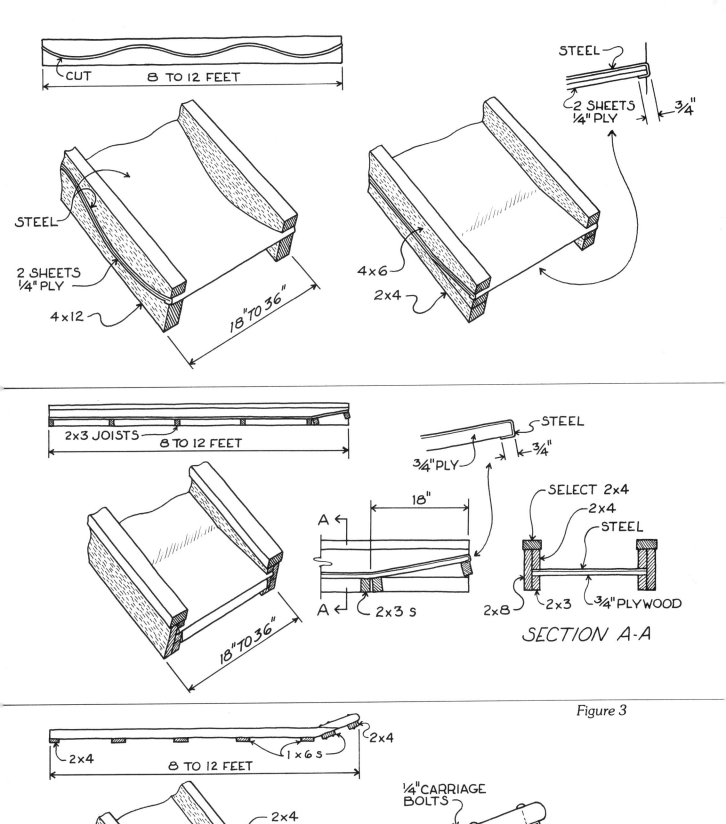

CUT 8 TO 12 FEET

STEEL

2 SHEETS ¼" PLY 3/4"

STEEL

2 SHEETS ¼" PLY

4 x 12 18" TO 36"

4 x 6

2 x 4 18" TO 36"

2 x 3 JOISTS 8 TO 12 FEET

STEEL

¾" PLY 3/4"

SELECT 2 x 4
2 x 4
STEEL

18"

A

A

2 x 3 s

2 x 8 2 x 3 ¾" PLYWOOD

18" TO 36"

SECTION A-A

Figure 3

2 x 4
2 x 4 1 x 6 s
8 TO 12 FEET

2 x 4

¼" CARRIAGE BOLTS

2 x 4

18" MAX.

31

BARREL SLIDES

The barrel slide is really not a slide at all, as children have very little exit speed. This equipment serves mainly to improve the child's awareness of body size. It also requires skill in controlling his descent and exit. For a greater challenge, ask the child to climb down and then up the barrel slide without using his hands.

Fire Poles

Fire poles should not exit from decks that are more than seven feet from the ground and will actually function better from decks that are only four feet high. Very high fire poles can be used only by older children, and they can perform only the simplest of moves like gripping and sliding down. When the pole descends from a lower deck, many creative moves become possible. One of the most popular is to take a run at the pole, grab it, and spin around while descending.

Balance Beams

The balance beam is intended primarily as a tool for increasing dynamic balance ability and can also be used as an element in constructive play. Initial moves on the beam consist of walking forwards, backwards, and sideways. Static balance activities include the one-foot balance, the one-leg squat, and the jackknife (sitting on the beam while raising both legs). The difficulty of these moves can be increased by using the narrowest edge of the beam, moving the beam higher, or placing it at an angle.

Ramp Boards

The ramp board, like the balance beam, will frequently be a part of constructive play. It can also be used in conjunction with the sawhorse as the start to a vault. Younger children can use the ramp as a slide, if it is smooth enough, or as a climbing device.

Rings and Trapezes

After the age of seven, children lose interest in the standard swing. It can then be replaced with rings or a trapeze bar.

There are many moves which can be performed on this equipment to develop arm, hand, and upper torso strength. Simple swinging motions and releases are the earliest maneuvers. Pull-ups and pull-overs can be done when enough practice has developed arm strength.

Once the child is able to pull up and rest his midriff on the trapeze, he is ready to go over it and land on the opposite side. A similar move called skin-the-cat involves grasping the bar with palms forward, bending over and lifting the feet off the ground, and then drawing them under the bar to come around gently back to the ground.

Ladders and Tire Climbers

Children develop climbing skills at a surprisingly young age, actually before they have good judgment about risks. Parents should monitor children's climbing to be certain that they do not get into trouble.

Climbing develops strength and coordination, but its most important contribution to child development is the improvement of motor planning skills. The child must imagine how to get from point A to point B and evaluate the difficulty of the tasks involved.

In a properly designed play structure it should not be more difficult to climb down than to climb up. This is true of standard rung ladders but not of the kind of step ladder attached to most slides. We have all seen a child stuck at the top of a slide because of inability to back down the ladder and fear of going down the slide.

The tire climber is slightly more difficult than a regular rung ladder because the tires vary in firmness of support. This makes it more difficult for children to anticipate exactly what movements and adjustments will be required before actually beginning to climb.

HORIZONTAL LADDERS

The horizontal ladder develops two major areas: upper torso strength and coordination. Initial use of the ladder involves just hanging from it to develop grip strength. The first steps include moving forward with the dominant hand then leading with either the right or left. Soon a coordinated rhythmic pattern develops that includes swinging the body back and forth to build up momentum. At this point the child begins to skip rungs. Asking the child to go across backwards or with his eyes closed also increases the level of difficulty.

Bridges

Bridges connect one part of the play structure with another. The tire or suspension bridge develops foot-eye coordination and depth perception and improves postural security and balance.

The rope bridge, whether it be an intricate web design or simply several lines strung between two points, demands a higher level of skill and agility. Asking the children to move across backwards, sideways, and with their eyes closed also will increase their skill.

Turning Bars

The turning bar must be adjustable, or more than one bar must be provided. For the young child, simply lying over the bar helps establish an awareness of the body's middle. He can perform movements like skin-the-cat and pull-overs at a height of about five feet. (*See Rings and Trapezes*.) At seven feet it can be used by older children for pull-ups and a variety of gymnastic moves. (*See Bibliography.*)

Parallel Bars

Few pieces of equipment develop upper arm strength as well as the parallel bars. The first step is simply to support his weight with stiffly extended arms. Next, the child should try to move his body forward by alternately sliding each hand ahead and then try moving backwards.

Another skill involves swinging the body back and forth and then using this momentum to propel it forward. The "saddle travel" requires the child to sit on the bars, lean forward and take a grip in front of his legs, raise up, and swing his legs up and round in front.

Ropes

Ropes are a terrific way to develop the upper body. The only problem is that sliding down ropes produces a bad burn. Therefore, it is important that this skill be developed slowly so that the children have the strength and ability to come down the rope hand-over-hand. Tie the rope to the safety rail at the top of the slide and let the rope hang down the chute. This will give the kids an inclined plane to pull themselves up.

Warn children that they must *never* tie or even pretend to tie the rope around their own bodies or that of another child.

For older children the rope may be suspended from a horizontal support. Early exercises include chinning and lowering the body from a standing position to a supine position and raising it again. Regular rope climbing should start with just the arms, and lifting only a few feet off the ground. The child should practice until he can climb about four feet high and come back down hand-over-hand without dropping or sliding. Finally, he can try climbing the rope with it locked between his feet.

Hammers and Nails

The hammer and nails used to construct the adventure play area require a high degree of hand-eye coordination and strength. Until the age of six, kids cannot nail without

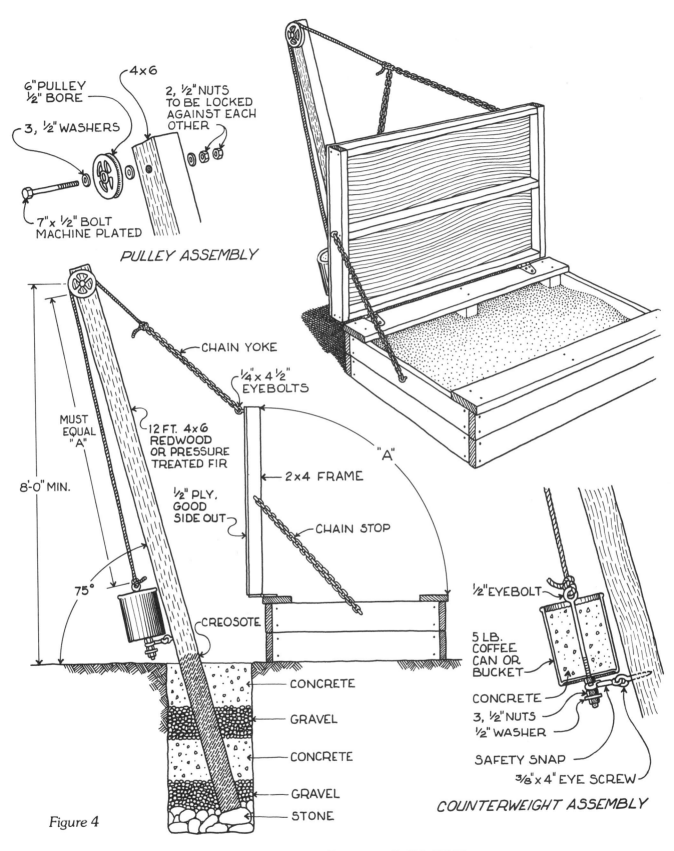

6" PULLEY ½" BORE

3, ½" WASHERS

4×6

2, ½" NUTS TO BE LOCKED AGAINST EACH OTHER

7" x ½" BOLT MACHINE PLATED

PULLEY ASSEMBLY

MUST EQUAL "A"

8'-0" MIN.

CHAIN YOKE

¼" x 4 ½" EYEBOLTS

12 FT. 4×6 REDWOOD OR PRESSURE TREATED FIR

2×4 FRAME

"A"

½" PLY, GOOD SIDE OUT

CHAIN STOP

75°

CREOSOTE

CONCRETE

GRAVEL

CONCRETE

GRAVEL

STONE

Figure 4

½" EYEBOLT

5 LB. COFFEE CAN OR BUCKET

CONCRETE

3, ½" NUTS

½" WASHER

SAFETY SNAP

⅜" x 4" EYE SCREW

COUNTERWEIGHT ASSEMBLY

SANDBOX COVER

Figure 5

using both hands, and it is only after age eight that their wrists have the kind of rotation which permits true hammering. Nonetheless, children can nail with some success from age five. Using soft woods like pine and drilling a small hole first can help. The idea is for the skill to be practiced successfully enough to keep the child motivated.

Sandboxes

No other feature of the child's environment begins to compare with the sandbox for play value. A small investment in time and money returns thousands of hours of creative play. Sand's most attractive characteristic is that it allows children to build roads, make castles, bake cakes, and generally create an infinite variety of play experiences. For all of its great features, sand does have some drawbacks. However, a little care and planning can minimize these problems.

SANITATION

Figure 4 shows a sandbox with a counterweighted cover. This is the ultimate solution for keeping sand clean. After investigating many other designs using canvas, plastic sheeting, or rollaway covers, this one appears best if you must cover your sand. Its main advantage is the ease with which the box can be opened and closed. Other designs may work well for a few weeks or months, but unless the box can be covered easily in a few seconds, one day it will be left open. This defeats the entire purpose of the cover, because once the sand is fouled there is little point in covering it.

For a larger sand area, the design can be built twice as big. You also may wish to place the sandbox so that the lid acts as a windbreak or shade.

Covered sandboxes are needed under trees or in neighborhoods with many cats. Some people have had success with spray that repels cats, and families with aggressive dogs do not have too much of a cat problem.

If you don't need to cover the sandbox, you can use any of the designs shown in Figure 5.

TYPE OF SAND

The sand you buy must be clean. If any soil or clay remains, these very fine particles bind the sand together and it will pack very hard, making play difficult. Sand that has been screened to keep particles between size 10 and size 20 seems to be best. Sand larger than size 10 begins to lose its ability to hold shapes and thus does not work for constructions such as castles.

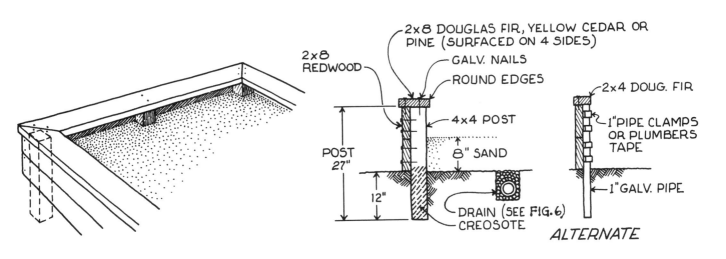

2×8 DOUGLAS FIR, YELLOW CEDAR OR PINE (SURFACED ON 4 SIDES)

GALV. NAILS

ROUND EDGES

2×8 REDWOOD

4×4 POST

POST 27"

8" SAND

12"

DRAIN (SEE FIG.6)

CREOSOTE

2×4 DOUG. FIR

1" PIPE CLAMPS OR PLUMBERS TAPE

1" GALV. PIPE

ALTERNATE

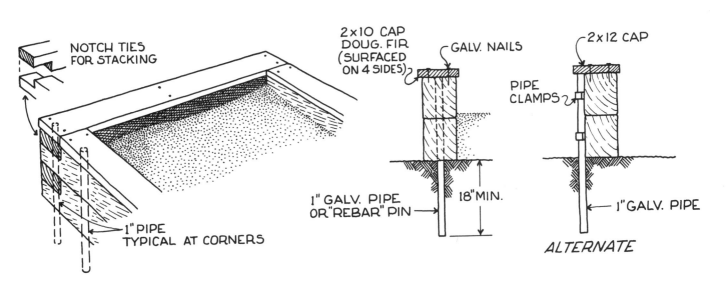

NOTCH TIES FOR STACKING

2×10 CAP DOUG. FIR (SURFACED ON 4 SIDES)

GALV. NAILS

1" PIPE TYPICAL AT CORNERS

1" GALV. PIPE OR "REBAR" PIN

18" MIN.

2×12 CAP

PIPE CLAMPS

1" GALV. PIPE

ALTERNATE

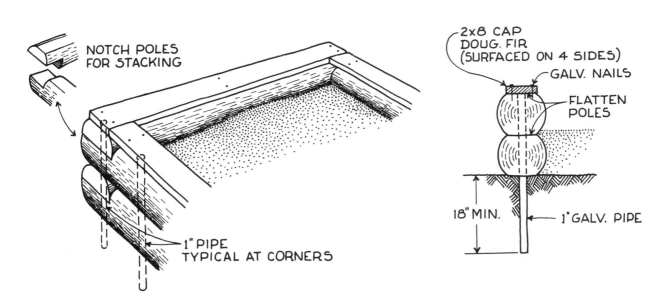

NOTCH POLES FOR STACKING

1" PIPE TYPICAL AT CORNERS

2×8 CAP DOUG. FIR (SURFACED ON 4 SIDES)

GALV. NAILS

FLATTEN POLES

18" MIN.

1" GALV. PIPE

INSTALLATION

A cubic yard of sand—three feet wide, deep, and high—contains twenty-seven cubic feet of sand. We strongly recommend spreading the sand eight inches deep. Therefore, one cubic yard of sand will cover thirty-six square feet (approximately six feet by six feet). A cubic yard of sand weighs 1.3 tons, so build the sandbox where it will not be too difficult to fill.

With the sand eight inches deep, it is unlikely that you will have any problems with drainage. However, if the soil underneath the sand is pure clay, you may want to install a leach pipe. (*See Figure 6.*) Drainage is important because the sand must be kept moist if it is to function well as a play material. Dry sand does not have much body, while moist sand is *excellent* for retaining the shapes a child constructs. A water source near the sand area would thus be a good idea. The ideal might be to have a hose that runs just a trickle, so that the kids can channel their "river" all around the sandbox.

SAND TOYS

Children will play contentedly for hours with nothing but sand, but small toys greatly improve the quality and duration of this play. Unless you provide sand toys, the children will find their own. Tools from the garage, electric trains, fine china figurines, and other inappropriate objects may find their way into the sandbox.

Plastic is the best material for sand toys. Some aluminum objects may also function well but wood and steel toys do not last very long in a wet and abrasive environment. The best sand toys—such as plastic kitchen utensils—are bought not at a toy store but at the hardware store. (*See Figure 7.*) Some plastic cars or dolls are also suitable and not many are required. Remember to select toys which are not sharp and do not present a major hazard if a child should fall on them.

Eventually all of the sand toys will get lost or wear out. They become lost very quickly

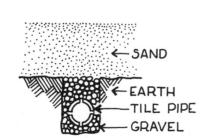

Figure 6

SAND

EARTH

TILE PIPE

GRAVEL

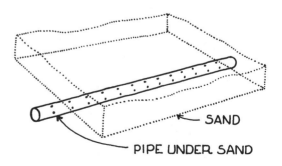

SAND

PIPE UNDER SAND

DRAIN

Figure 7

unless you provide well-designed storage. Open shelves right next to the sandbox are the best; stout wooden boxes may also be used. These boxes will work better if you drill holes in the bottoms or replace them with heavy wire screen to let the sand fall through.

The children should be strongly encouraged to put their toys away before they come inside. This training should not be too difficult if started at an early age. By the time the kids are seven, it's very difficult to get them to clean up after themselves.

When you periodically clean up the sand area and put away the toys, it is wise to take inventory and determine what needs to be replaced. Such sandbox housekeeping is essential. Without it, the level of play activity will dwindle to nothing within a few months.

There is a whole school of child therapy based on the use of sandboxes and small toys. This simple and natural approach to working with children has great significance. Children can easily show emotional relationships in their lives by using toys, whereas words come only with difficulty. Daily access to a well-equipped sandbox gives the child a potent projective tool with which to work through problems.

To enhance this kind of play, the selection of sand toys should be very rich and detailed. Collect small houses, trees, Lego blocks, dishes, dollhouse furniture, shells, ceramic figures, plastic animals, dolls representing family members, and other miniature toys. Open shelving and periodic housecleaning become absolutely imperative with such a large number of small items.

Your children's sand play could be a completely private event, but to get the very most out of the sandbox, you should share the world they create. Instead of simply calling the kids in at dinnertime, take a few minutes to go out and see what they have been doing. Just spending ten or fifteen minutes a day listening to their fantasies will put you in very close contact with your children.

Listening uncritically, asking a few questions, and trying to understand what your children are communicating, will be very satisfying to all. The sandbox will create a communication bridge, and your children will be able to tell you things that would be difficult, if not impossible, without it. A few minutes' attention every day, or even every other day, will also encourage your child to create more elaborate constructions.

Ground Cover Retainers

In my earlier discussion on safety, it was noted that a fall-absorbing material is required under all play equipment. Sand, gravel, or wood chips were recommended as the best materials for this purpose. Without some kind of retainer, these loose materials will quickly spread away from the play structure and lose their value as a fall cushion. The following discussion of ground cover retainers focuses on sand, since it is the best ground cover, but the ideas apply equally to other materials.

Fall-absorbing ground covers must be at least six inches deep, though eight inches is preferred. With this depth, children will seldom dig down to the subsoil and mix it with the ground cover. Eight inches of sand provides plenty of material to build mounds and castles without creating bare spots. Of course, sand dumped on the ground will not stay in place, so some sort of retainer is necessary.

The most attractive—and in some ways the simplest—retainer is a shallow depression surrounded by grass, much like a sand trap on a golf course. The only difficulty is in contouring the ground. This is very hard work and may require earth-moving equipment. Also, drainage must be provided since the sand will be lower than the surrounding grass.

If sunken sand areas are adjacent to walkways, some kind of curb is needed between the walk and the sand. While concrete, brick, and stone make attractive curbs, their use should be discouraged because of the hazard such hard edges present when children fall.

Wood is the best material to retain sand because it is much less apt to injure a falling child. Yet wood may rot where it comes in contact with soil or sand. A concrete curb with a wooden cap is perhaps the ideal solution. However, this is both technically difficult and expensive.

Wood can be treated to resist bacteria, moisture, and insects. Pretreated wood is available in most lumber yards because it must be used where the frame of a building joins its foundation. After this material is cut to length, the ends of the board should be given an additional application of coppernate (a trade name for the copper salts used for preserving) because the original pressure treatment may not have penetrated to the core of the board.

Redwood and cedar have a natural resistance to decay and are used frequently. However, even redwood may decay unless it is of high quality and should be chemically treated where it is likely to contact soil or moisture.

All rot-resisting treatments are toxic and must be handled with extreme care. They

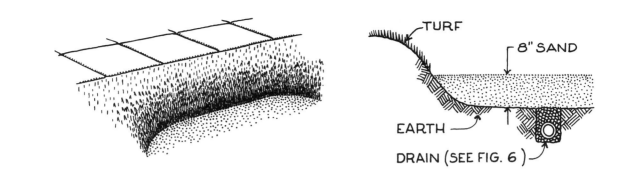

TURF

8" SAND

EARTH

DRAIN (SEE FIG. 6)

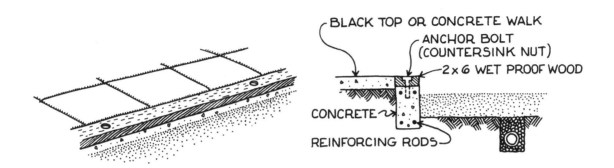

BLACK TOP OR CONCRETE WALK

ANCHOR BOLT (COUNTERSINK NUT)

2 x 6 WET PROOF WOOD

CONCRETE

REINFORCING RODS

Figure 8

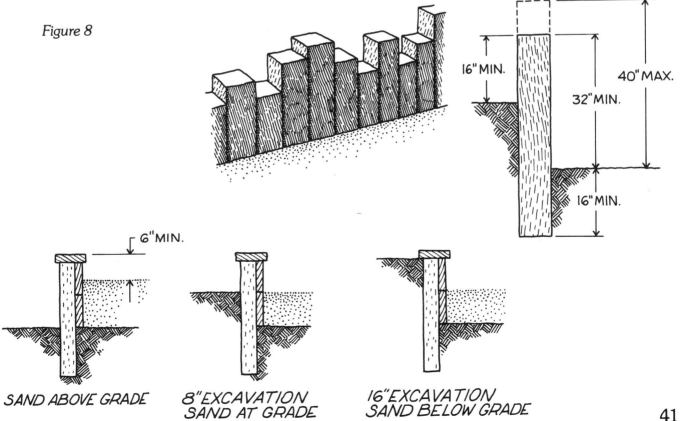

16" MIN.

40" MAX.

32" MIN.

16" MIN.

6" MIN.

SAND ABOVE GRADE

8" EXCAVATION SAND AT GRADE

16" EXCAVATION SAND BELOW GRADE

41

must be applied cautiously, and children should be kept away until the treatment has soaked into the wood.

In addition to treated, redwood, and cedar lumber, telephone poles and railroad ties are occasionally used as sand retainers. Often these recycled materials are in bad condition, but they can be cleaned effectively with an industrial-quality disk sander. Fresh wood cuts may require additional preservative.

In general, unless the poles or ties are obtained free, they are not worth the enormous amount of time and energy expended to make them clean and smooth enough for a child's play area. The materials are heavy and difficult to handle, and using a disk sander is hard and somewhat dangerous work. Creosoted ties and poles usually "weep" when warmed by the sun. For all these reasons, ties and poles are not recommended for the play area even though their rugged appearance might be aesthetically interesting.

Swing Frames and Attachments

As we have seen in earlier pages, swings do have a function in the play area. The swinging motion stimulates the balance system and is pleasing to children, and learning

Figure 9

how to pump promotes some motor development. If a swing is to provide a valuable experience over a long period, the simple to-and-fro style should be combined with other, more advanced, types. The tire swing is interesting to children over a wider age span and can also be used by several children at one time.(*See Figure 1.*)

The swinging motion creates very strong forces on a swing frame (*Figure 9*). Not only must the frames be sturdy, they must also be firmly secured to the ground or they will

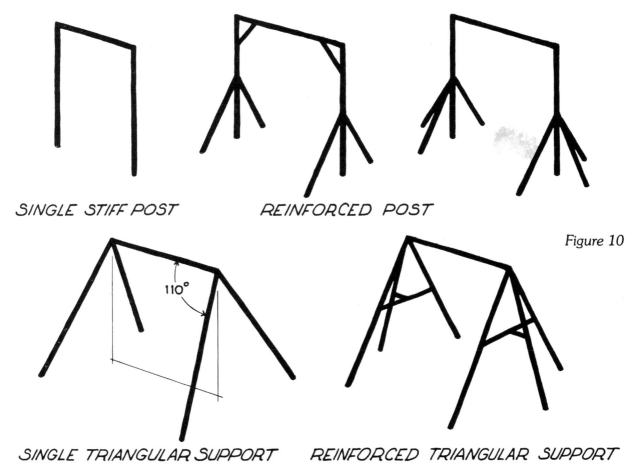

SINGLE STIFF POST   REINFORCED POST

Figure 10

SINGLE TRIANGULAR SUPPORT   REINFORCED TRIANGULAR SUPPORT

43

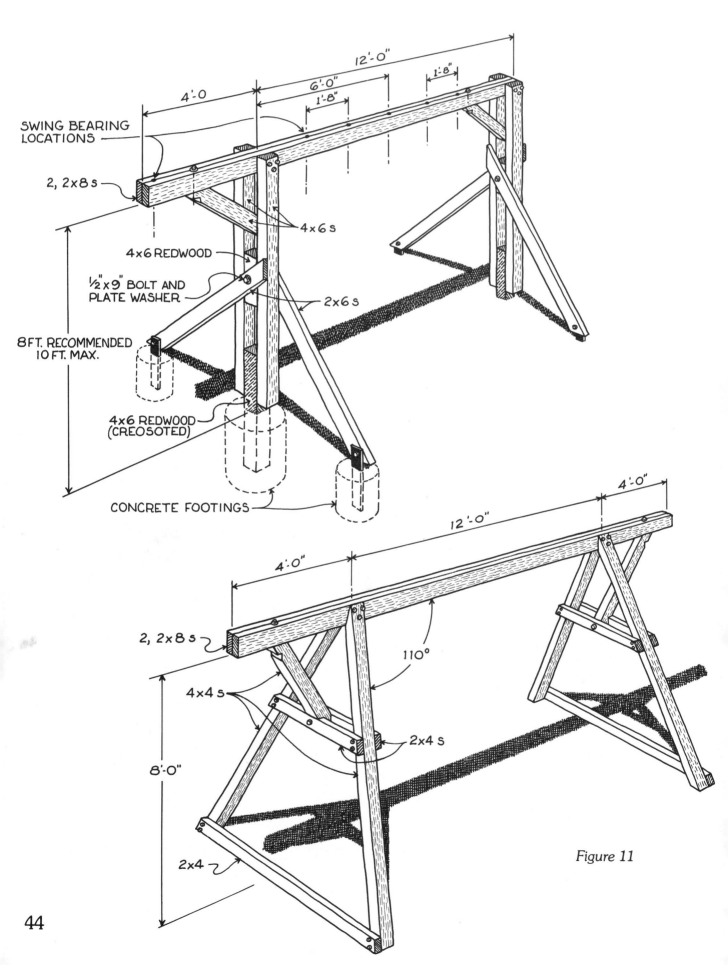

SWING BEARING LOCATIONS

12'-0"

6'-0"

4'-0

1'-8"

1'-8"

2, 2x8 s

4x6 s

4x6 REDWOOD

½"x9" BOLT AND PLATE WASHER

2x6 s

8 FT. RECOMMENDED 10 FT. MAX.

4x6 REDWOOD (CREOSOTED)

CONCRETE FOOTINGS

12'-0"

4'-0"

4'-0"

2, 2x8 s

110°

4x4 s

2x4 s

8'-0"

2x4

Figure 11

44

tend to move. The stresses created by the swinging motion cause the joints of the swing to work loose and become unsafe. For this reason, the swing frame must be carefully constructed. **Periodic inspection of the swing is absolutely essential.**

Either wood or metal may be used to build frames. Wood is the first choice unless you have access to metalworking equipment and desire twenty-year durability. Wooden structures may be constructed from massive elements or from smaller pieces of lumber properly reinforced (*see Figures 10, 11, and 12*).

Wood, by nature, is a flexible material, and some movement of the post and crossbar is inevitable. This flexing of the wood is acceptable if it is not too severe. Be certain, however, that the movement is actually a slight bending of the wood and not a movement of the joints, as this will become steadily worse.

When left to their own devices, children will spontaneously invent a swing which is very different from an adult's version. Instead of hanging the swing from a crossbar, children will tie a rope, as high up as they can reach, between any two convenient points. (*See Figure 13.*)

This swing acts very differently from the traditional to-and-fro swing. First of all, it is very difficult to ride. A child may practice for several weeks before he is able to stay on the rope for more than a few minutes. Kids find this swing exciting because they are always falling off. This actually makes the swing safer than the adult version because the child must be constantly alert.

The kid's version also eliminates another problem of the traditional swing. It has a very narrow arc, which means that there is less danger from flying feet and that there will be less of a hole under the swing in which water can collect. The kid's swing can be integrated into a small area and made part of a total play environment while the traditional to-and-fro swing should be set to one side, away from traffic which might collide with the rider.

Few children younger than five will be able to use the kid's swing because of the skill required. Therefore, smaller children will need a different type of swing. For them, the tire swing is best.(*See Figure 1.*) Not only can the tire swing do everything that a to-and-fro swing does, it can also spin around. Nothing is more exciting to kids than spinning, and several recent studies indicate that children who pursue this kind of activity at an early age show improved motor performance over children who do not.

There is one problem with spinning, however: the supporting ropes may twist and pinch fingers. While no serious injury will result from such a pinch, some parents may

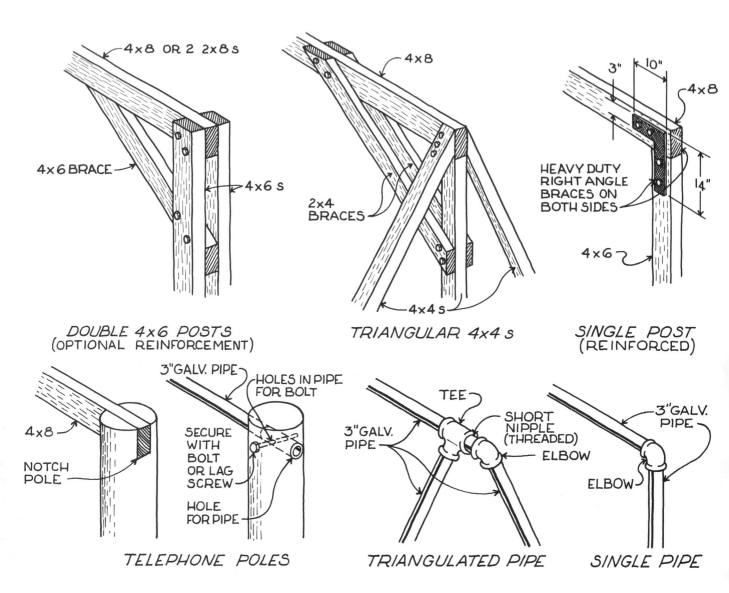

Figure 12

wish to eliminate the possibility. This can be done by including a swivel as part of the swing bearing. You may choose to keep the tire swing simple and easy to build or opt for more safety.

If you include a standard swing in your play yard, you must find a soft, belt-type swing seat. The old-fashioned wooden swing seat can cause many injuries. Accidents may occur when the unoccupied swing is swung into a child's head. Soft, lightweight swing seats may be ordered from Child Life (*see Materials*). The telephone

Yellow Pages should list several suppliers of playground equipment who can provide you with a soft swing seat. Such a seat, as well as others, can be made very easily. (*See Figure 14.*) You might even make a pretty good swing from a loop of large rope, omitting the seat entirely.

Shown in Figure 15 are several swing bearings. Any of these will be adequate for most backyards. If you anticipate heavy use, then the hardened eye, hinge, or a commercial bearing would be advisable. All of the wear in swing bearings occurs in the small

Figure 13

Figure 14

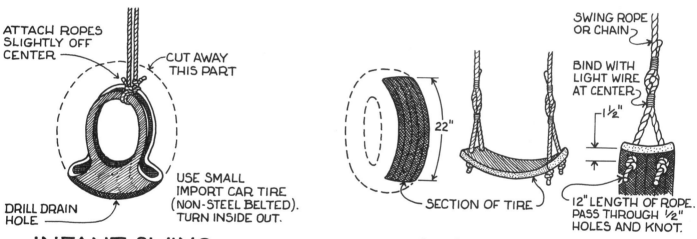

ATTACH ROPES
SLIGHTLY OFF
CENTER

CUT AWAY
THIS PART

DRILL DRAIN
HOLE

USE SMALL
IMPORT CAR TIRE
(NON-STEEL BELTED).
TURN INSIDE OUT.

INFANT SWING

22"

SECTION OF TIRE

SWING ROPE
OR CHAIN

BIND WITH
LIGHT WIRE
AT CENTER

1½"

12" LENGTH OF ROPE.
PASS THROUGH ½"
HOLES AND KNOT.

STRAP SWING

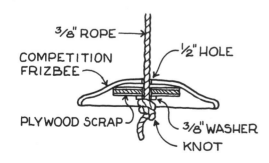

3/8" ROPE

COMPETITION
FRIZBEE

½" HOLE

PLYWOOD SCRAP

3/8" WASHER

KNOT

HEAVYWEIGHT
COTTON OR
BURLAP FILLED
WITH SAWDUST

MONKEY SWINGS

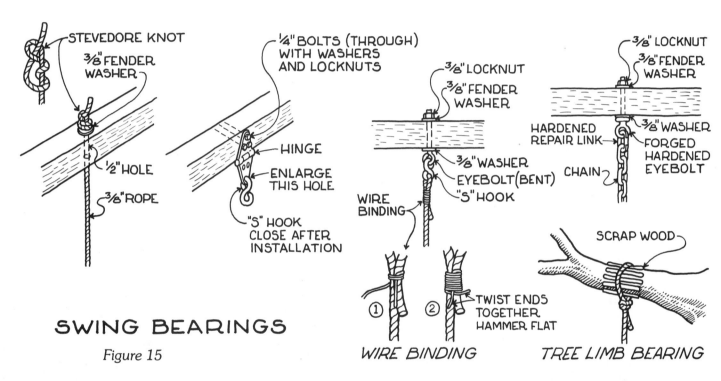

STEVEDORE KNOT
3/8" FENDER WASHER
1/2" HOLE
3/8" ROPE

1/4" BOLTS (THROUGH) WITH WASHERS AND LOCKNUTS
HINGE
ENLARGE THIS HOLE
"S" HOOK CLOSE AFTER INSTALLATION

3/8" LOCKNUT
3/8" FENDER WASHER
3/8" WASHER
EYEBOLT (BENT)
"S" HOOK
WIRE BINDING
① ②
TWIST ENDS TOGETHER HAMMER FLAT

3/8" LOCKNUT
3/8" FENDER WASHER
HARDENED REPAIR LINK
3/8" WASHER
FORGED HARDENED EYEBOLT
CHAIN
SCRAP WOOD

SWING BEARINGS

Figure 15

WIRE BINDING   TREE LIMB BEARING

area where the last link of the chain contacts its rigid support. With frequent use, especially by children over sixty pounds, the S-hook linked to an unhardened eye bolt will wear completely through in a few months. The swing bearing must be inspected often for such wear and upgraded if it needs replacement more than once a year.

The Tarzan swing is another kind designed by kids. (*See Figure 2.*) This is simply a rope hung from any tree limb. The feature which makes this swing exciting is the length of the ride. For this reason, the higher the supporting tree limb, the better. Kids will al-

ways find a way to create an elevated takeoff point. Frequent strategies include stacking boxes, borrowing a ladder, and climbing another tree. Recognizing this pattern, the play environment might have a takeoff station.

The perfect swing is a Tarzan swing on a big limb which hangs out over a pond or swimming hole. These days a child will be lucky to find such a swing even at summer camp. On your next camping trip or summer picnic, take along a length of rope in the hope of creating such a great swing experience.

CONSTRUCTIVE PLAY COMPONENTS

The Constructive Play Area consists of loose parts and a combination playhouse/storage shed. If you are concerned with your backyard's appearance, you will want to locate the Constructive Play Area in an unobtrusive corner. If this is not possible, the area can be screened by fences and the storage shed itself can act as a partial visual barrier.

More than fifty types of loose parts are suggested for use in the Constructive Play Area. Clearly, it would be unrealistic to have all of these items. Storage space alone would require the area of a two-car garage. However, the list that follows provides many alternative materials which serve essential play functions. Most of these objects can be gathered at little or no cost. Obtaining a half dozen items from each of the three categories—Play Furniture, Play Tools, Play Supplies—will be a good beginning for the Constructive Play Area.

The Constructive Play Area is an extension of the sandbox. The Adventure Play Area described on pages 110-11 builds even further on this concept. It may take several years, starting with a simple sandbox and a few sand toys, then adding more loose parts and storage, and finally providing materials for a total play environment created by the children themselves. This process of developing loose materials for constructive play will promote very intense play activity by your children. Without any other play equipment, these simple components will occupy them totally.

It should be noted, however, that the Constructive Play Area will not provide for all of your children's play needs. Motor play, in particular, is lacking. If your children participate in swimming or gymnastic classes, these activities will compensate for the lack of motor play activity provided in the Constructive Play Area.

The more flexible the material, the more play value it has. Thus, sand and water have high play value, and concrete has very low play value. Portable components such as sawhorses and walking boards are more flexible than fixed play structures and, therefore, have greater play value.

One might consider loose parts as toys, but they actually go far beyond the frivolous connotation of toys. An object becomes more than a toy when it can be used in many different ways to accomplish the child's own goals. Loose parts are less toys than tools for play. They facilitate, improve, and augment the child's activities. After the children have grown up and moved away, you may find that these playthings are still being used around the house.

Because these objects can be useful for years, it is good economy to build them as well as possible. Use screws instead of nails, select better grades of materials, and weatherproof them. Be careful not to make the units so heavy that a child cannot move them.

After you have determined which components and how many of each you will be creating, give some thought to storage. Whether you use prefabricated storage or your own design, make sure that each piece of equipment has its place and that any object can be easily withdrawn when everything has been properly stored. All too often, storage sheds are useless because the materials the children want are so far in the back, or under so much other stuff, that it's not worth the effort to get them out. During play, children may not even know that they want a particular object if they don't see it. "Out of sight, out of mind," is especially true for kids.

The storage shed itself can become part of the children's play environment. It should be designed to be both storage shed and playhouse. The shed will have long-term utility, for example, to store garden equipment or lawn furniture. For that reason, it, too, should be well constructed of long-lasting materials. In addition, it should be designed with skids on the bottom so that it can be relocated when no longer needed for play activities.

A trip to a government surplus store will reveal dozens of potential loose parts of real value, and garage sales often yield intriguing odds and ends. There is something whole-some about finding common objects which can be transformed into tools for play instead of routinely acquiring the expensive, breakable, materialistic junk sold in stores as toys.

The following lists of loose parts—play furniture, play tools, and play supplies—are not exhaustive. Rather, the selection has been based on the experience of day care centers, nursery schools, and homes. All of the items are basic equipment in early childhood education facilities and have proven to be durable, flexible, and to maintain a high interest level.

Play Furniture, such as sawhorses or boards, creates environmental focal points alone or in combination. Moving these objects around creates spaces which become the settings for dramatic play. These objects are fairly permanent and will retain a high level of play value over a long period for children of many ages.

Play Tools, such as hammers or hats, are durable items which facilitate the children's play. Many of these objects are used for role playing. One might consider these objects to be toys, except that they can be used in a wide variety of situations under the creative control of the child, while toys generally require the child to adapt his play to specific use situations.

Play Supplies, such as paint, glue, and nails, are used up during play and must be replaced periodically. While parents may find this inconvenient, such supplies are very important to children. Play supplies are the glue of the whole Constructive Play Area.

Play Furniture

Figure 16

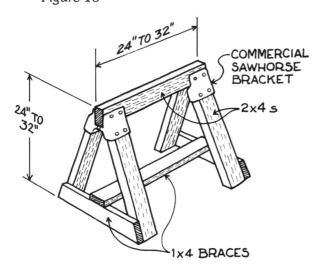

SAWHORSES

Hardware stores carry metal sawhorse brackets which fit 2 x 4s. You can build sawhorses without using these brackets, but this requires a very high degree of craftsmanship. Even with the brackets, braces for the legs are recommended to keep the devices rigid. This extra strength is needed because the sawhorse is the base for many heavy loads, some of which having a moving component. For example, the sawhorse, when combined with a walking board, makes an excellent teeter-totter. At least two horses should be built, although four would be better. If they are going to be used by small children, then they can be as low as eighteen inches. In general, however, a better height would be twenty-four inches to twenty-eight inches.

MILK BOTTLE CASES

In the old days, the milkman used to deliver glass bottles of milk in a wooden box with a wire bottom. Nowadays, milk no longer comes in glass, but it is still moved around in cases. These cases are now plastic, but they are just as durable as the old wooden ones. The cases, found at dairies, can be used to store sand toys. They can also be stacked up to create all kinds of structures, especially when combined with walking boards or pieces of plywood, and used as furniture in playhouses. Although they are seldom free, these cases still are an excellent investment.

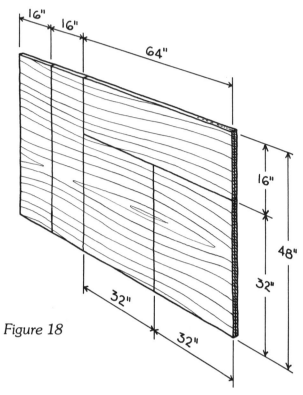

Figure 18

4 FT. x 8 FT. SHEET OF ¾" PLYWOOD
CUT FOR CONSTRUCTIVE PLAY

WALKING BOARDS

Walking boards can be used for ramps, decks, balance beams, and even slides. When raised at both ends by a concrete or wood block, they can be used as trampolines. These boards must be strong and lightweight. Regular one-inch lumber is too weak, and two-inch lumber is too heavy. The best material for these boards is "stair tread." This is a special lumber for stair construction and is a little thicker than the regular one-inch material. It is made of kiln-dried, straight-grained fir, which makes it very strong. It comes in two widths, with the narrower generally preferred for backyard use.

The boards should be no shorter than six feet nor longer than ten feet. It is essential for safety that these boards have a small strip of wood glued and screwed on both ends to act as a cleat, preventing the boards from slipping off their supports. The walking boards should be protected with several coats of clear plastic finish.

ASSORTED PIECES OF PLYWOOD

These can be used much the same way as walking boards, but are never over five feet long. They can be of random size, cut to the pattern shown, or cut to a size which best fits the structure you are going to build. Five-eighths-inch and three-quarter-inch plywood are the best thicknesses. Be certain that the plywood is for exterior use. Shop-grade plywood is good enough, although it is less available than "good one-side" plywood. Take special care to round off all the edges, then paint it with a quality sealer and a color or clear varnish. Here, again, cleats are advised on the ends of the boards, although these may be attached with glue and nails.

Figure 17

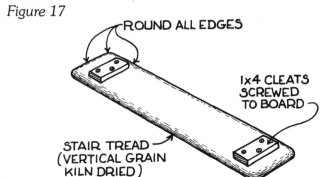

ROUND ALL EDGES

1x4 CLEATS
SCREWED
TO BOARD

STAIR TREAD
(VERTICAL GRAIN
KILN DRIED)

CABLE SPOOLS

Wire, cable, and rope are all shipped on spools, and businesses that use or sell these materials are good sources for free spools. Look in the Yellow Pages under wire rope. The kids use these spools as furniture and sometimes as wheels.

LADDERS

Small, portable ladders are essential for climbing and can be used as building components. A good size is six feet long and eighteen inches wide. The side rails are best made from 2 x 3 fir and the rungs from closet pole or 1 x 4 fir glued and screwed in place. As with the walking boards, a cleat should be attached at either end.

SMALL STEP LADDERS

Used as a climbing or a construction element, a small, two-step ladder can function either as a regular ladder or as a sawhorse. With younger children especially, the step ladder should be locked into an open position by nailing a 1 x 4 on each side between the legs. The ladder will last much longer if painted or varnished.

CONCRETE BLOCKS

While not appropriate for young children, concrete blocks can be used very successfully by children six years and older. A few blocks are useful and the kids can put to use as many as two dozen in all sorts of constructive activities. The blocks have enough weight and good, flat surfaces so that they will stay put and not topple over. The only problem with concrete blocks is that they are abrasive and have sharp edges.

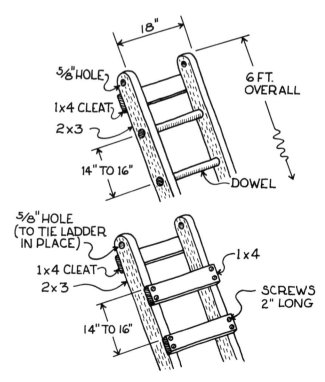

Figure 19

53

BARRELS

Barrels come in many sizes, shapes, and materials. Both wooden and metal barrels make excellent construction components. The wood in wooden barrels expands and contracts with moisture and thus requires tightening now and then. This is done by driving the barrel hoops downward toward the center of the barrel. Painting wooden barrels reduces the tendency to take in water and helps to stabilize the shrinkage.

Metal barrels can have sharp edges. In most large towns there are companies which sell used barrels. Often these businesses can roll the open end of the barrel to create a smooth edge. This can be done to both ends of the barrel to make a crawl-through tunnel. Buckets and kegs are also very useful and can often be obtained at no cost.

CONCRETE SINKS

Used sinks are very inexpensive. The best ones for the play area are the deep concrete utility sinks. These can be set up on blocks just high enough so that the water used by the kids can be channeled off into the garden through a drainpipe. Fill the sink with a hose.

WOODEN BOXES

Wooden boxes should be reinforced with 1 x 4 cross braces or plywood corners. Smaller wooden boxes are also very useful and may be found at businesses which import fragile products. Check the Yellow Pages under importers or large furniture stores. Additional nailing to strengthen the boxes and painting to waterproof them may be required.

TREE STUMPS

Kids use short lengths of trees as building blocks and furniture. Although very heavy, they are still movable because they can be rolled.

Some woods, particularly pine, will seep pitch from the cambium layer just below the bark, making it sticky all around the top of the stump. Once fully dried, this will no longer occur. (The aging process takes a year or less for most woods.) Painting the cut ends with wood preservative will extend the life of the stump, but for longer resistance to decay, the bark must be stripped away and the whole stump treated. Tree sections can be located through tree trimming services and firewood dealers.

LONG POLES

Poles are useful for making tepees and tents. They can also be used as construction elements. A diameter of two and a half to three and a half inches is best, as the poles must be both strong and light, and six to nine foot lengths are most useful. The harder and more flexible woods are preferable. The bark should be stripped off to impede decay and insect damage. Wood lot owners who thin out small trees are an excellent source of these poles.

ASSORTED PLASTIC CONTAINERS

A visit to the housewares section of any hardware store will reveal plastic containers in every conceivable shape and size. Plastic wastebaskets, planter barrels, and storage boxes are excellent for the play area. The smaller containers can be used for storage and the larger ones can actually become construction elements.

USED TIRES

Two or three tires can be used in the Constructive Play Area. Too many tires become rather unsightly, so try not to collect more than needed. Tires can be found free at any gas station or tire retreader. Kids seem to prefer motorcycle tires, hot rod slicks, tractor tires, and airplane tires to car tires. Giant earth-grader tires are also available. These are excellent for sandboxes because they do not rot, are soft to fall on, and are free.

To make them more useful as sandboxes, enlarge the center hole with a knife. A linoleum knife with a hooked blade which is sharpened on a whetstone will work best. Use water as a lubricant. While it may take several hours and a strong arm to open up an earth-grader tire, the resulting sandbox will be very satisfactory. Remember to drill holes in all the tires for drainage. Few things are more unpleasant than stagnant water in the bottom of a tire!

SNOW FENCING

This is an inexpensive fence material with wooden slats held in place by wire. Kids can use a couple of ten-foot lengths of this fencing to define various spaces within the yard, and to create jails and other areas.

BEANBAG CHAIRS

Quality beanbag chairs are relatively waterproof and very durable. These are perfect for the play area and provide a soft element which is difficult to obtain in other ways.

LADDER BOXES

As the ladder box is set on its different sides, its function changes. As shown in the illustration, it can be used as a child's first horizontal ladder. Turned on end, it makes a puppet theater or make-believe store. Set flat, it can be a lion's cage or part of a constructive play environment. Add a piece of canvas and it makes a great fort.

Figure 20

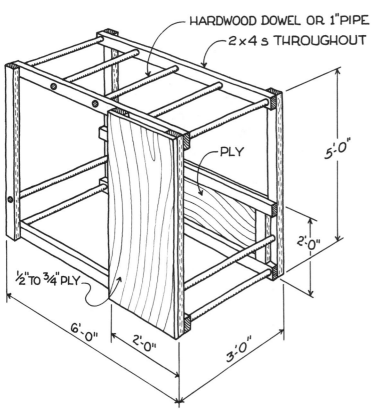

HARDWOOD DOWEL OR 1"PIPE

2×4 s THROUGHOUT

PLY

5'-0"

2'-0"

½" TO ¾" PLY

6'-0"

2'-0"

3'-0"

Play Tools

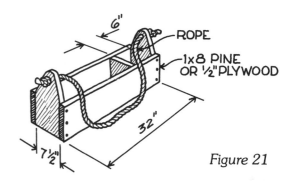

6"

ROPE

1×8 PINE OR ½" PLYWOOD

32"

7½"

Figure 21

TOTE BOXES

A tote box is essential for keeping tools together and it must have certain dimensions. The box should be long and narrow so it can be carried like a suitcase, and it cannot be too large or it will be heavy and cumbersome.

HAMMERS AND HAND TOOLS

For young children, a hammer is the only tool that is truly functional. Until the age of seven most children lack the coordination or mental ability to use tools such as screwdrivers. A toy hammer is too light and soft. Nothing could be a greater turnoff for the developing craftsman than a useless toy hammer. While most adult hammers are too heavy, there is a middleweight hammer intended for women. It weighs about ten ounces and is perfect for kids.

The combination of soft pine, sturdy galvanized nails, and the proper weight hammer will allow even the fairly young child to hammer successfully. A clear demonstration of hammer technique is needed. Such instructions as: "focus and concentrate on the head of the nail," "use only one hand," and "swing with the whole arm, not just the wrist," are helpful so long as the parent is patient and understands that the child will be able to master only one aspect of the skill at a time. It may take as long as a year of practice before the child will be able to integrate all of the motor skills involved in hammering.

After the kids have shown some ability with hammering, other tools can be introduced, like a heavy-duty, plastic-handled screwdriver. It must be strong because it will be used as a prying tool and a chisel, seldom as a screwdriver. A pair of pliers is also appropriate. The best kind does not have the adjustable slip-joint feature which allows it to be opened for large objects but which only frustrates children. A saw can be introduced only after the children have become fairly proficient with tools.

A work bench with a vise, or clamps that fit on sawhorses, is essential for safe and successful sawing. The best saw is a garden pruning saw which folds into its handle. These saws tend to stay sharp longer and make a wide cut which prevents binding. Their folding feature makes them safer and protects the teeth during storage. You must instruct the children in how to lock the saw open and start a cut.

Another useful and safe children's tool is the surform. This modern invention is a cross between a file and a plane. It is used for shaping wood and rounding edges. As with all cutting tools, it will get dull, so the blades must be replaced occasionally.

SHOVELS

Here again, adult shovels are too big and toy shovels are too small. You can find trenching shovels at army surplus stores, and these are a perfect size.

GARDEN HOSES

The right length of garden hose just reaches from the faucet to the play area, with a little room to spare. The kids should have their own so that it is always handy. The smallest diameter, one-half-inch, is best, and it should be of a good quality so that it can be handled easily even when cold. A flow restricter at the faucet will control the volume. There are also timers which will turn off the water after a predetermined period. These will pay for themselves in a short time. Providing water to the play area efficiently and reliably is one of the most important aspects of developing a functioning play space, so select and set up the hose with care.

Figure 22

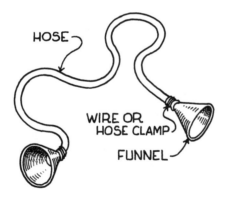

TALK TUBES

The talk tube is the child's telephone. It stimulates imaginative play and language development. Talk tubes can be installed permanently or left loose. An old garden hose can be fitted with a plastic funnel at either end. ABS or PVC plastic pipe can channel sound around and through a play area.

FANTASY OBJECTS

In the section on sand toys, we presented a list of equipment for sand play. Other common objects can be added to increase the inventory of props used in imaginative play. Plastic or aluminum kitchen utensils and dishes can be used for domestic play. Aprons, hats, and shoes form costumes. All of these items should be selected with consideration for safety. Therefore, they should not be sharp and should break away easily.

The props need not be many, but they should be durable and tolerate wetness without damage. Therefore, rubber boots are better than old shoes, plastic hats are better than cloth, and polyester (fireproof) capes and aprons are better than cotton. A government surplus store will provide a wealth of materials, especially dials and controls. An old toaster-oven makes a great play oven. A trip to a Salvation Army Thrift Store will yield a bounty of sturdy fantasy play materials.

MIRRORS

A mirror is very useful in generating fantasy play. The mirror must be plastic or stainless steel to be safe. You can buy one in a toy store or make one by using spray glue to attach a sheet of mirrored Mylar to a piece of tempered Masonite.

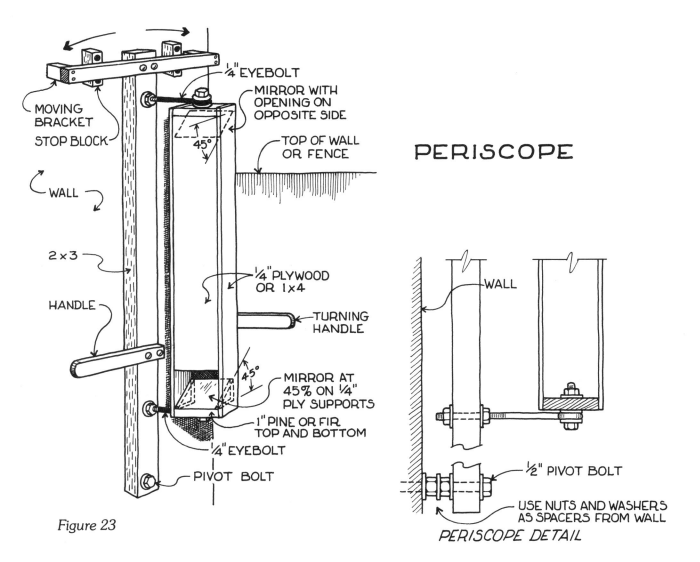

MOVING BRACKET

STOP BLOCK

WALL

2×3

HANDLE

¼" EYEBOLT

MIRROR WITH OPENING ON OPPOSITE SIDE

TOP OF WALL OR FENCE

45°

¼" PLYWOOD OR 1×4

TURNING HANDLE

45°

MIRROR AT 45% ON ¼" PLY SUPPORTS

1" PINE OR FIR TOP AND BOTTOM

¼" EYEBOLT

PIVOT BOLT

PERISCOPE

WALL

½" PIVOT BOLT

USE NUTS AND WASHERS AS SPACERS FROM WALL

PERISCOPE DETAIL

Figure 23

PERISCOPES

A periscope requires some construction but is really worth the effort as it will be a central feature in much fantasy play (*see Figure 23*).

INNER TUBES

Kids can use regular car inner tubes as furniture, as cushions to sit or jump on, or as parts of games. Inner tubes provide a soft element in the play space, are durable and inexpensive, and are, therefore, very highly recommended.

WHEELED VEHICLES

The new plastic tricycles like the "Big Wheel" are superior to the old metal variety. They are lower and therefore less apt to tip over, and the low seating position builds more leg development than the erect position of the traditional design. These trikes are quite durable and the kids certainly prefer them. Now, if they could only be more quiet, they would be perfect!

Every kid needs a wagon to haul stuff. Also, small two-wheeled garden wheelbarrows are perfect for kids.

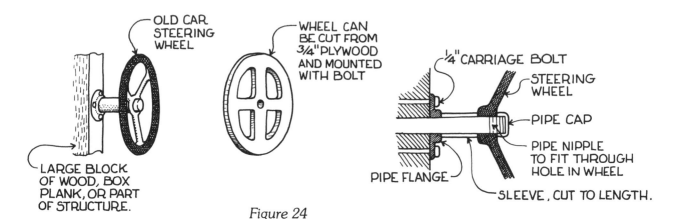

Figure 24

STEERING WHEELS

Perhaps no other single feature stimulates fantasy play as effectively as a steering wheel. One can be permanently placed with a cluster of dials and controls or mounted on a box so that it can be moved from place to place. Steering wheels can be found at any auto wrecker's or cut out of three-quarter-inch plywood.

TOYS

Large plastic cars and trucks can be used by kids of all ages. It is a mistake to think that when kids reach the age of five they will want to get more advanced toys. Be sure the wheels and axles are sturdy and, preferably, nonmetal.

FLASHLIGHTS

We buy kids all sorts of toys that require batteries, yet seldom do we get them the one toy that is the most magical. A flashlight makes the inside of a box or tent more exciting. It should be made of waterproof plastic with a button as well as a sliding switch. Tape over the sliding part so that the child must press the button to turn on the light, and the batteries will last a very long time. This modification can also be made on some lanterns.

SUITCASES

An old plastic suitcase is good for both fantasy play and for storing costumes. Remove the lining and fit a simple closing device on the outside, as kids find the normal locks neither durable nor useful.

PULLEYS

A pulley or a wooden block and tackle are useful if they are the right size to match the rope. The top of the pulley should have a safety locking hook so that it can be easily attached.

SOFT STUFF

Bungee Cords are heavy elastic bands with hooks on each end. Kids find them very interesting and use them to temporarily attach odd-sized objects.

A hammock is a simple and inexpensive way to create an interesting play zone. Kids are not always active, and the hammock provides a focus for relaxation.

Kids can use pieces of canvas to create tents and other spaces. They are most useful if they are of a durable, middleweight fabric. Hem the edges to prevent tearing, and put grommet holes along the edges so they can be tied in place with rope or Bungee Cords. Tie-dyeing adds an element of color and is a project many kids enjoy.

Play Supplies

CARDBOARD

Cardboard can be used to create all sorts of spaces and objects. It can be cut easily with a pocketknife or keyhole saw, and held together with filament tape. You can pick up large appliance boxes free at many stores. Kids can decorate them with crayons, wide felt-tip pens, and water-base paint.

After a period of use, or after a rain, the cardboard has to be replaced. While supplying cardboard requires some time and effort by parents, it is one of the best investments that can be made in providing constructive and creative activities for the kids.

SCRAP LUMBER

Wood is essential in any of the serious building that kids will do. Very young children need small pieces of soft pine as it is nearly impossible to pound a nail into harder woods like fir. Such soft wood can be found at a shop where patterns for metal castings are produced. You can find packing boxes at many businesses which engage in shipping, and housing construction also produces large amounts of scrap lumber.

BRICKS, STONES, AND PEBBLES

These are readily available and make good objects for constructive play.

ROPE, TWINE, AND STRING

Rope should be provided in several sizes and types. Lengths from eight to twenty feet are best. All of the larger sizes, from three-fourths-inch down to three-eighths-inch, should be of supple plastic. None should be smaller than three-eighths because children may fall when attempting to support their weight on a lighter rope. Secure the ends of the rope with a knot so that they do not unravel.

Twine or string, which are too weak to hang from, should be cut into lengths of less than twenty-five feet and wound onto sticks. This prevents whole balls of string from being wasted at one time in a massive snarl. For making attachments, clothespins are a good addition, as are S-hooks.

NAILS

Nails used by kids must be galvanized so they will not rust. There are two types of nails: box and common. Common nails are better for children because they are thicker and less apt to bend. This advantage of extra strength is slightly offset by the extra force required to drive the common nail and its increased tendency to split wood. But, all things considered, the most common problem kids have is bending the nail.

Be sure to buy quality nails. Some imported nails are so soft even experts can't drive them. Provide several different sizes: two and a half inch (ten penny), two inches (six penny), and roofing nails. Two pounds of each, stored in coffee cans, should be enough to get your kids started.

WHEELS

Building your own go-cart is one of the highlights of childhood. Making a car go and steer is a real engineering feat; learning how to make brakes is even harder. However, a car can't be built without wheels. Old trikes, baby carriages, wagons, etc., are good sources for wheels. Also, try to provide some kind of axle, preferably one which can be nailed in place. Wheels are useful only if they can be easily attached to a vehicle.

PIPES

Children are fascinated by pipefittings. Short lengths with elbows and T shapes will be used for all kinds of constructive activities. Metal pipe is best but is very expensive. The new PVC plastic works very well. The joints of plasticpipe fit very snugly, so sanding the ends of the pipe segments reduces their diameter and makes them easier to assemble.

MISCELLANEOUS

Other odds and ends can be useful. Polyethylene sheeting can be used to make tents, or cut up and stapled or taped in place for windows. Kids find endless uses for assorted tin cans and plastic bottles, and burlap bags are a favorite for storing or hauling gear.

IV
Play
Structures

Getting Started

The core of the backyard play area should be a large sandbox with lots of loose parts. The addition of a well-designed play structure can greatly expand the kinds of activities your children will enjoy and increase the length of time they use the play area. This is particularly true of children over four years old who seem to benefit the most from play apparatus.

The most common error adults make when creating play spaces is to think that swings and a slide will entertain their kids. The result is an expensive piece of equipment that gets used only occasionally. The addition of movable parts allows children to modify their play space and thus greatly expands its usefulness.

While a backyard play area of sand and loose parts can function well without a play structure, a structure cannot function well without the loose parts. Therefore, when choosing your structure and planning your budget, be certain to set aside enough funds for both the structure and the purchase of sand and movable components.

The success of a good play space will be enhanced if you think of the backyard play area as one which will grow and change over the entire span of your child's formative years. Ideally, the kids will do much of the modification themselves. When children take control over their environment, changing it to reflect their own needs, they create an emotional connection that is essential to a strong self-concept and sense of competence. This "place bond" is also the stuff of which memories are made. Think back to your own childhood play areas and you will quickly understand the importance of this emotional attachment.

The play structures which follow will provide for your child's physical development and act as a focal point for fantasy play. The structure which most emphasizes the motor aspect of play is called the Junior Olympian.

The section on using the equipment explains in detail the function of the various attachments and suggests ways they can be used to build strength, coordination, and agility. Of course, any of the features of a particular design could be added to other structures, so you are advised to read that section even if the design you select does not have all the features listed. Without some knowledge of the functions and benefits of all the attachments, it would be difficult to appreciate their value to the kids and they might be overlooked.

The Treehouse and the Adventure Play Area are environments which emphasize the imaginary qualities of play. They are really stages, and the loose parts are props for the children's games. These environments support long sessions of fantasy play during

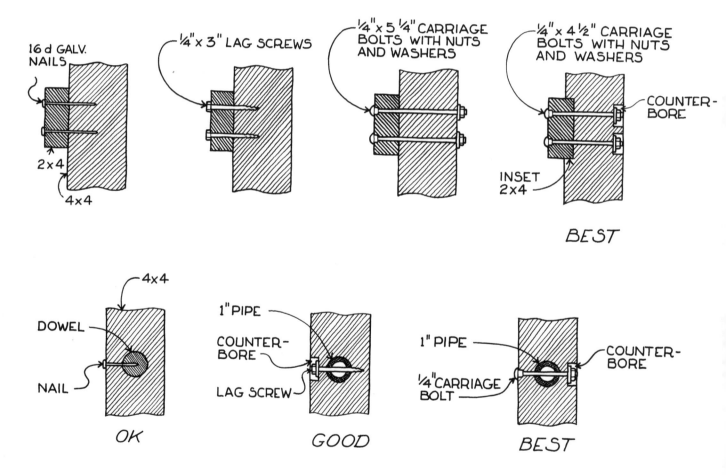

16 d GALV. NAILS

2 x 4

4 x 4

¼" x 3" LAG SCREWS

¼" x 5 ¼" CARRIAGE BOLTS WITH NUTS AND WASHERS

¼" x 4 ½" CARRIAGE BOLTS WITH NUTS AND WASHERS

COUNTER-BORE

INSET 2 x 4

BEST

4 x 4

DOWEL

NAIL

OK

1" PIPE

COUNTER-BORE

LAG SCREW

GOOD

1" PIPE

¼" CARRIAGE BOLT

COUNTER-BORE

BEST

Figure 25

FASTENING DETAILS

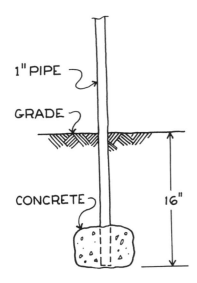

**FOUNDATION
FOR POLES**

1" PIPE

GRADE

CONCRETE

16"

which kids assign themselves roles and act out complex scripts.

The adult's role in the Junior Olympian structure is that of coach, teaching the children increasingly difficult movement skills. In contrast, the adult's role in the fantasy play environments is to restock materials and occasionally clean up.

The remaining designs combine various aspects of pure motor development and fantasy play. They introduce new building materials, are particularly well suited for phased construction, or are designed to be easily transported. People with design ability

should be able to combine any of those qualities in a structure uniquely suited to their child's needs. Parents who want very specific plans that can be followed exactly will find construction drawings for most of the structures.

The more complex structures can be built in phases. If you choose this method, it is important to make a schedule for completion of the various sections. Most of us have good intentions, but are often lacking in follow-through. Setting specific dates in the near future is one way of increasing the likelihood that the project will be completed. When working in phases, it is important to begin with the part of the structure that will be the most fun for the kids. If they really enjoy what you have accomplished, this, too, will encourage the completion of later stages.

Involving your children in the planning and construction of the play area is a sure way to guarantee its use. If you have a park or a good preschool in your area, a field trip will provide both you and your kids with examples of structures to discuss during the design phases. It will also give you new insights into your children's play patterns as you watch them on the equipment.

Remember, though, that the field trip is a unique experience and that the most exciting aspects of these play environments will seem the most attractive. Using a play area day after day is very different from enjoying a one-time visit, and you will have to adjust your observations accordingly. For example, the kids may want to play on only the circular slide and may ignore the sand area, yet, on a daily basis, the sand would actually get more of their attention.

You will be most successful in involving the kids if you can somehow make it appear that they discovered the whole idea. What a great learning opportunity, if they begin to feel responsible for the creation of their own play environment!

Develop a materials list and then take a trip to the lumber yard and hardware store. This will give your children meaningful lessons in economics which relate directly to their lives.

Once you've begun to get their involvement, the next trick is to keep it. This is harder than it sounds, because adults and kids have such different points of view. The parents want to get the job done, preferably in an efficient manner; the kids have to be able to enjoy the whole process or they get bored. Some of the construction can be tedious, and you will have to be careful not to expect too much from the kids. Remember that kids learn most by copying good role models, so it is valuable for them simply to watch you work. They may want to pound nails into scrap pieces of wood while they are watching. While this may seem pointless, it actually increases the speed with which they master the skills you are demonstrating.

The kids need not be involved with every aspect of the structure, but they must feel that they are really a part of what's happening. One good indicator that things are going well will be the good feelings generated between you and your children. You will also notice that their excitement and enthusiasm

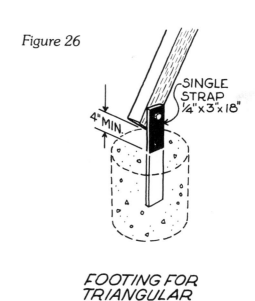

Figure 26

SINGLE STRAP ¼"x3"x18"

4" MIN.

FOOTING FOR TRIANGULAR SUPPORT

about the project, while it may not be constant, is strong and persistent.

The best way to be sure they feel involved is to really listen to your children's ideas and comments. This is not always easy, but responsive listening is the essence of being a parent. Expect their interest to ebb and flow—perhaps the most difficult aspect of working with children. The sign of a mature parent is the willingness to let things wait for a while and then pick them up again without bad feelings. Accept from the outset that you may not be able to keep to a predetermined completion schedule because the children come up with new ideas that should be followed.

Even though the kids' contribution will result in an environment which is different from the one you initially envisioned, their involvement will help to achieve the goal of making your backyard more interesting than TV.

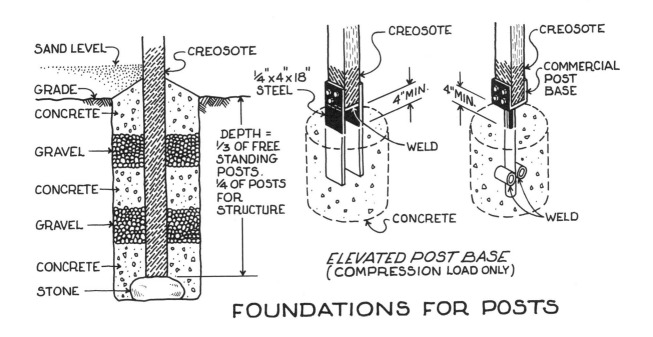

ELEVATED POST BASE
(COMPRESSION LOAD ONLY)

FOUNDATIONS FOR POSTS

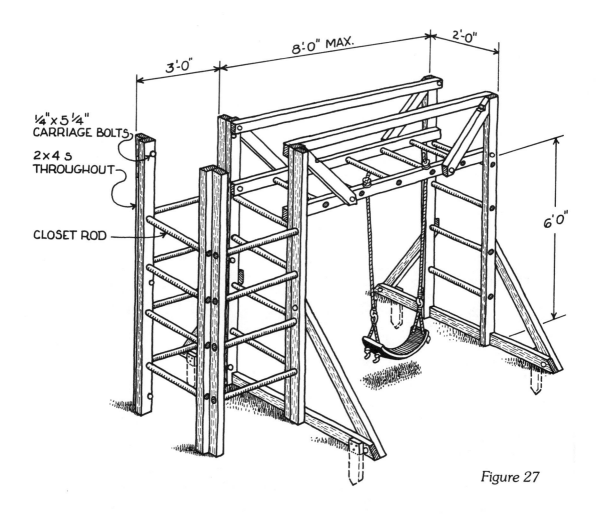

3'-0"

8'-0" MAX.

2'-0"

¼" x 5¼"
CARRIAGE BOLTS

2 x 4 s
THROUGHOUT

CLOSET ROD

6'0"

Figure 27

PORTABLE CLIMBER WITH SWING

This structure uses the most flexible construction system of any play structure design. The basic components are ladders, which can be combined in many ways to create a nearly infinite variety of structures. Use either standard 2 x 4s and closet rods or 2 x 3s and one-inch hardwood dowels to construct the ladders. These, in turn, are joined with one-quarter-inch carriage bolts, allowing simple disassembly of the structure. The units are also light enough that they can be moved around the yard with relative ease. Many of the designs described later in this book could be built with ladders as the main structural components.

The basic unit can be started by building only the swing frame, with the tower section added later. You can add more room for swings by making the support ladder longer. However, when the swing frame is made longer, it must also be made stronger. This can be done by adding two additional support beams to each edge, giving the effect of a 4 x 4. A 2 x 6 instead of 2 x 4 swing support ladder could span up to ten feet. Do not use 2 x 3s for this function as they are too weak.

The basic swing and tower could be expanded by adding another tower at the opposite end of the swing frame, or the tower can have two swing frames attached to it.

Supplying plywood sheets with cleats nailed on the edges, to act as platforms within the tower, will greatly improve the play value of the structure. Kids can attach smaller ladders with hooks cut on the ends to the rungs of the structure. Planks and sawhorses are also excellent loose parts that give this environment tremendous play potential. A detachable slide board can also complement the unit. Use canvas to cover sections of the tower for a clubhouse feeling.

While this system of construction with ladders is relatively inexpensive and non-technical, it does have certain limitations. One of the best features of the system is its lightness, which makes it convenient to move around. This lightness can also be a drawback, because the units will not have the inherent stability of structures built with more massive components.

Thus, you must consider the number and size of children who will be using the equipment when you choose the ladder system. The lateral forces this unit will withstand are also lower than for designs which employ footed supports. This, in turn, means that fewer moving components, like swings, can be attached.

Ladders are great for climbing — an essential feature of any play environment. However, the modular aspect of the ladders limits the variety of climbing experiences available on the structure. Often the "ladderness" of the system gets in the way of other play functions. For example, this system does not make a particularly good fort.

In general, the ladder system works best where portability is a very high priority. It creates structures which are best suited for younger children, and only a few children at a time. The addition of appropriate loose parts will greatly improve the play value of the basic ladder structure with tower and swing.

Two Ways to Build Ladder Section

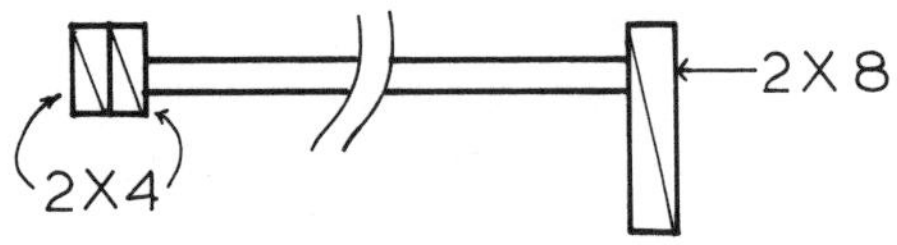

2 X 8

2 X 4

PORTABLE CLIMBER

End View

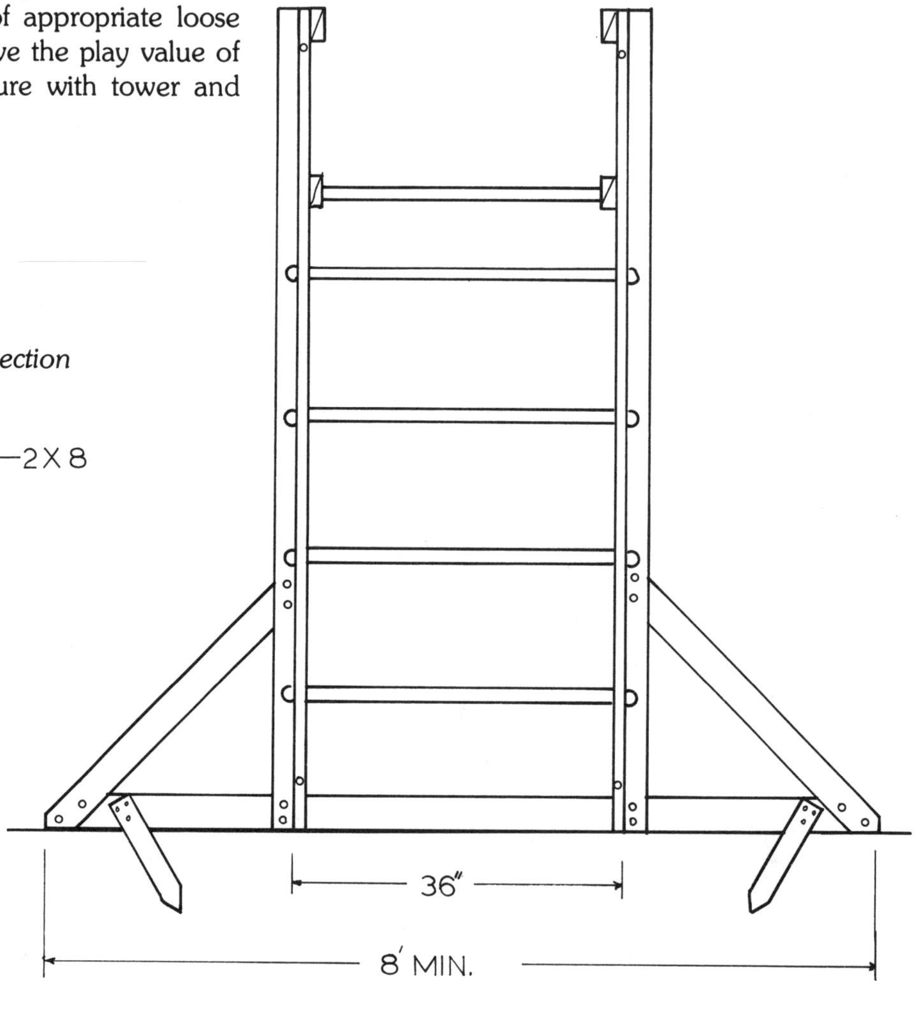

36"

8' MIN.

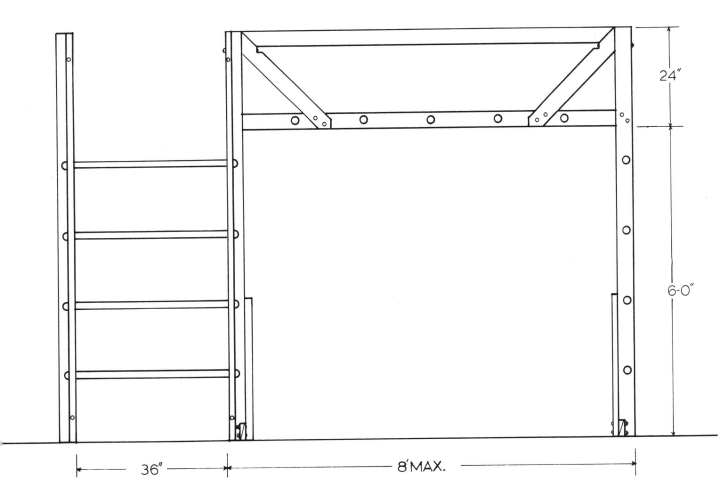

24"

6-0"

36"

8'MAX.

PORTABLE CLIMBER *Side View*

73

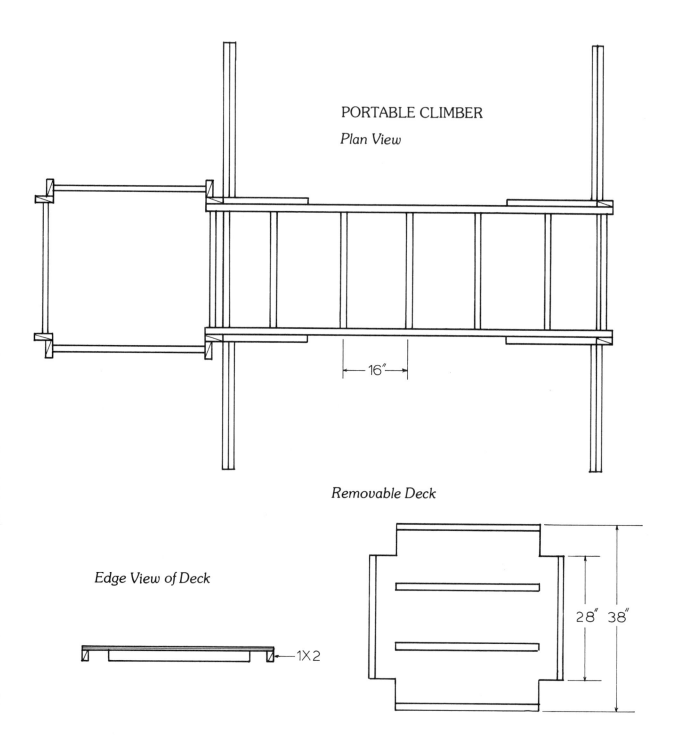

PORTABLE CLIMBER

Plan View

16″

Removable Deck

Edge View of Deck

1X2

28″ 38″

CLUBHOUSE

One of the things kids need most is a place to call their own. The first real building project most children undertake is a fort or clubhouse. Parents try to fill this need with a playhouse. The trouble with the grownups' ideas about playhouses is that they are usually simple boxes with a roof, a door, and maybe a window. Such a playhouse is boring, and it requires a particularly creative child to convert it into an environment where real play can happen.

Instead of thinking of a clubhouse as a miniature house, think of it as a stage set for dramatic play. Raising the activity above ground level greatly stimulates play activity and creates a basement crawl-under space. Building more than one level is also helpful, and attachments like banister slides and fire poles add to the creative potential. Fantasy play props, like steering wheels, add yet another dimension.

A totally enclosed play space is really not what children usually seek. One of the major shortcomings of the traditional playhouse is that it is so enclosed that it is actually confining.

Each backyard has its own special conditions, and the location of the structure within the backyard is important. In general, the more open the site where the structure is located, the more enclosed the structure needs to be.

Figure 28 shows a clubhouse which is as open as possible. This unit ought to be located in a well-defined and relatively private area, preferably under a tree. If it will be built in an exposed area, then it will need to be made more enclosed. For example, it should have a roof if it is not built under a tree. A tent made to fit the structure could add to the sense of enclosure.

A swing frame would complement this design and the total play value of the area. The frame could be fitted with swings for younger children and gymnastic apparatus for older children. The entire structure could be set in sand, providing both a play medium and a fall cushion. The clubhouse is the lowest of all the designs presented and, therefore, is least hazardous in terms of falls.

The design shown here is fairly small, requiring an area of approximately two hundred square feet. By removing the lower platform it could be made even smaller, without destroying the integrity of the overall design.

The unit can be built quite inexpensively with a wide variety of materials salvaged from other uses. If plywood is used for walls, it is best to cut openings in the sides for observation ports. These can be simple squares and circles or you can experiment with graphics and color. In a similar fashion, additional cloth side enclosures could be

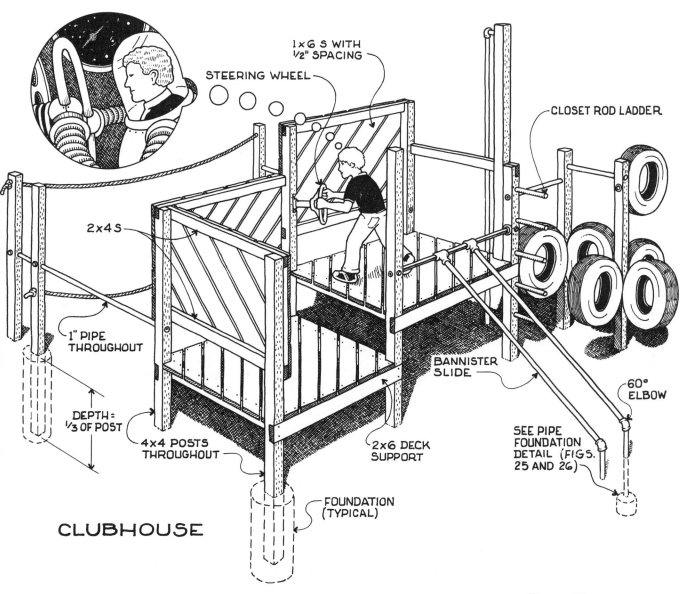

1×6 S WITH ½" SPACING

STEERING WHEEL

CLOSET ROD LADDER

2×4 S

1" PIPE THROUGHOUT

DEPTH = ⅓ OF POST

4×4 POSTS THROUGHOUT

2×6 DECK SUPPORT

BANNISTER SLIDE

60° ELBOW

SEE PIPE FOUNDATION DETAIL (FIGS. 25 AND 26)

FOUNDATION (TYPICAL)

CLUBHOUSE

Figure 28

made from old sheets or tie-dyed canvas with the edges hemmed and grommets added for fast removal.

A collection of five to ten plastic milk cases would make a perfect addition to this structure. They can be used to carry play props and as furniture inside the clubhouse.

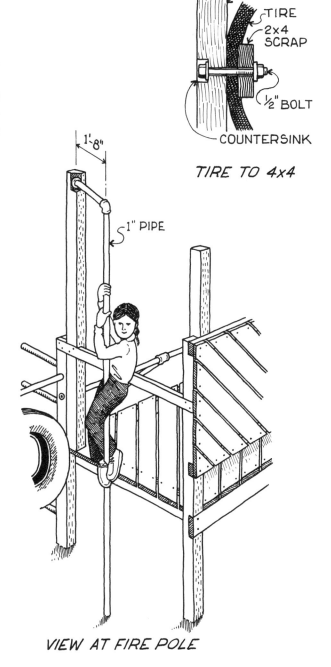

TIRE TO 4x4

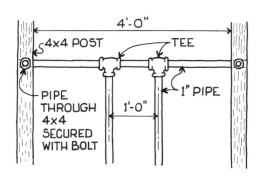

BANNISTER SLIDE DETAIL

VIEW AT FIRE POLE

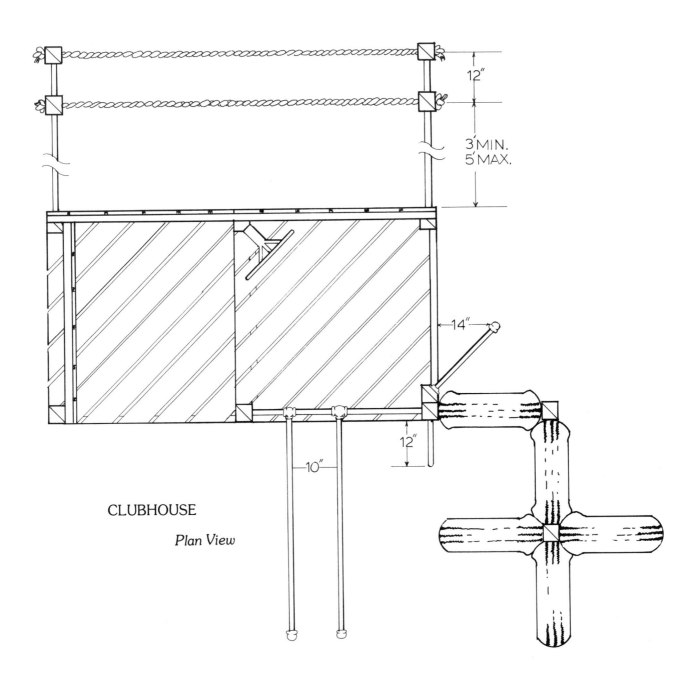

12"

3' MIN.
5' MAX.

14"

12"

10"

CLUBHOUSE

Plan View

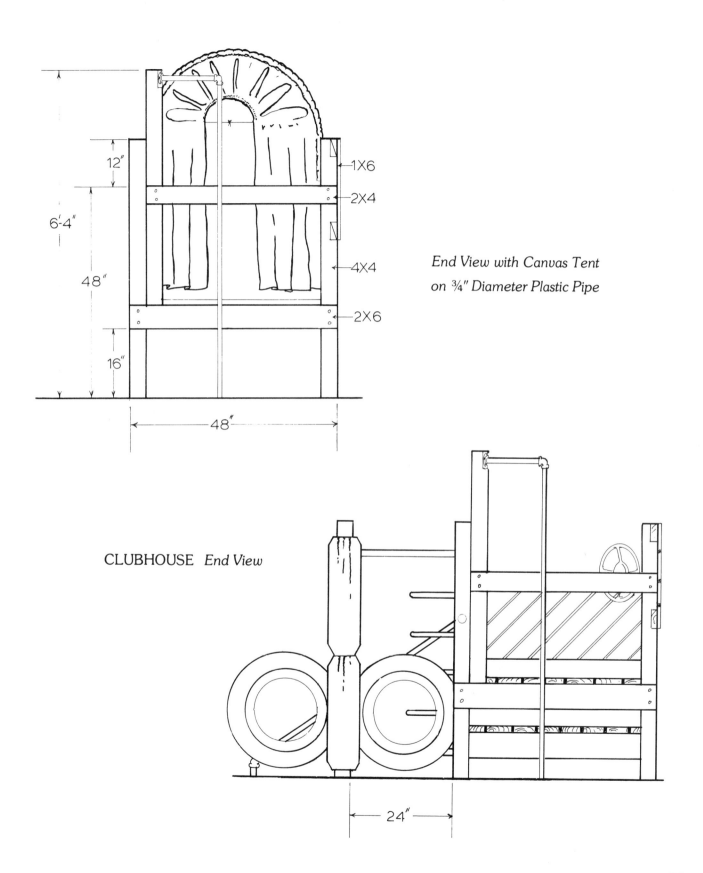

12″

6′-4″

48″

16″

48″

1X6

2X4

4X4

2X6

*End View with Canvas Tent
on ¾″ Diameter Plastic Pipe*

CLUBHOUSE *End View*

24″

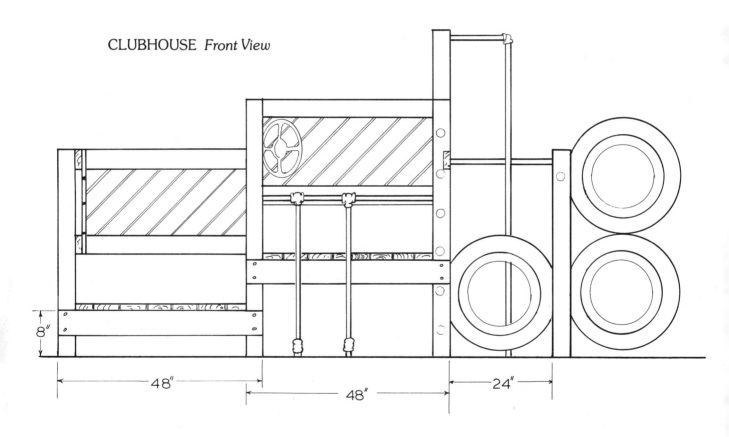

CLUBHOUSE *Front View*

TREEHOUSE

The instinct to build in the trees must be older than that of walking upright. Both gorillas and orangutans, man's closest animal relatives, build in trees. Most native peoples have great reverence for trees and may perceive spirits in them. Whether or not trees are homes for spirits or the ancestral heritage of *Homo sapiens*, no one can deny the special feeling a tree gives kids.

However, just being in a tree does not make a treehouse a good place to play. When grownups build them for kids, they often just make boxes and stick them up in the branches. Treehouses built by kids are invariably much more interesting and creative, but all too frequently they are structurally unsound. The best way to create an exceptional treehouse is to combine the creativity of the child with the building skill of the adult. One way to insure creativity is to select materials which harmonize with the tree itself, like limbs instead of 2 x 4s.

Trees seem very solid, and are indeed very strong, but strength is not the same as solidity. Trees move a great deal, even fairly close to the ground. This movement is caused by wind, and, at a much slower rate, by growth. This movement will break apart rigid structures, especially those of plywood.

A treehouse should "float" within the tree as much as possible. Taken to its logical conclusion, the structure could be totally suspended by chains, or lashed with rope.

The most successful approach is to attach one end of a board tightly to a limb. The other end of the board must be free to move slightly, or quite soon the nails will work loose or break. A fast-growing tree can actually push a board right off its nails in just a few years.

The most difficult part of the treehouse is the floor. This must support considerable weight and yet allow for movement. Attach the fundamental support elements with lag screws to insure adequate strength and elongate the holes in the beams through which these screws pass to allow for movement.

A combination of lumber and shingles works best for enclosing the treehouse. Abandon the notion of a roof and walls and simply construct enclosed areas. Use 2 x 4s for rafter-studs. Fix the top end securely with nails or lag screws and lash the bottom end. Make sure the ends of each side are parallel. Nail 1 x 4s between these ends at approximately twelve-inch intervals. Nail shingles to the 1 x 4s, making sure that the nails are not so long that they pass through the 1 x 4s and protrude on the inside. Shingles will not effectively shed rain if they are too close to horizontal. Make a pitch which will allow rain to run off the face of the shingles.

The shingle approach allows for a crazy and creative structure. The house could even be a dome shape with plastic bubble windows. It might have various rooms at spots where the tree will support them.

Unlike most other play structures, the treehouse should not have too many entrances. The best seems to be a rope ladder that can be pulled up after the kids are inside. A fire pole can serve as a secret exit, or you may be able to connect two trees with a rope bridge. This would make a great second entrance.

The illustration shows a cable ride coming off the tree house. These are available commercially (see Materials) or can be made with a pulley system. Because of the heavy loads these rides have to sustain, they must be inspected very often. Once a day during hard summertime play would not be too frequent. The slope of the ride should be gentle and should rise at the exit so that the children will have nearly stopped before they reach the rear support.

Treehouses have an almost mythological quality for children. If you were fortunate enough to have one as a child, you know what strong memories it created. While there are few things in a child's experience that are as powerful as playing in a treehouse, there are some aspects which should concern parents. Treehouses tend to be higher off the ground than other types of play structures, so parents should take extra precautions. To reduce the hazard from falls, parents should make a strict rule not to

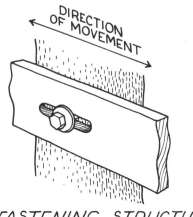

FASTENING STRUCTURE TO MOVING LIMBS

allow any objects to be left on the ground below the treehouse. Tree litter or fir bark must be spread thickly on the ground to act as a fall absorber.

A pulley system with a basket should be one of the earliest attachments. This will allow the kids to get stuff up into the treehouse without having to carry it, freeing both hands for climbing.

Talk with the kids about the potential of falls and teach them how to use the space safely to reduce the likelihood of a mishap. Your children should be made particularly aware of their responsibility for visiting friends. They should feel comfortable asking their playmates to observe your safety rules. It would not be out of place for you to have a few words with your children's guests before they are allowed to use the treehouse. As pointed out in an earlier section, it is an excellent idea to talk with the parents of any child using the treehouse, allowing them to inspect the environment and make their own judgment about whether or not their child should play there.

Figure 29

TREEHOUSE

83

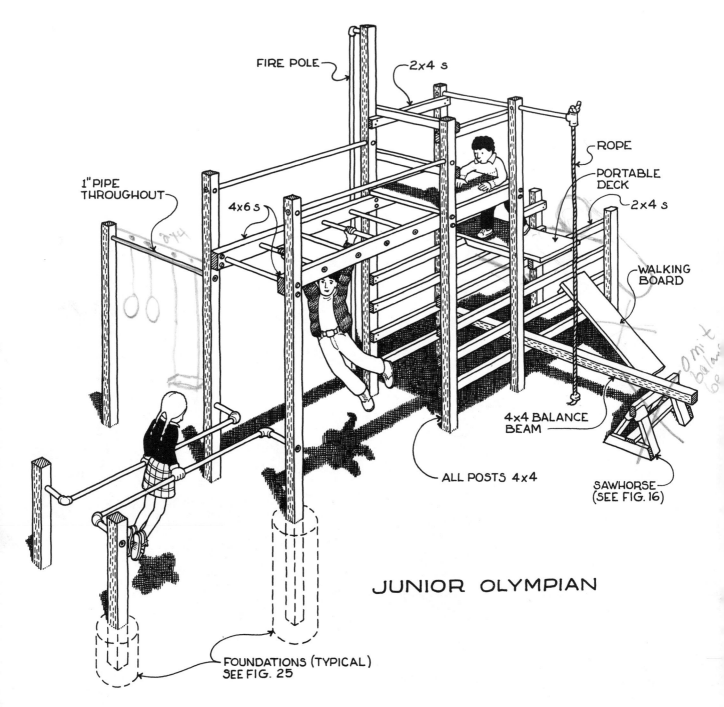

FIRE POLE

2x4 s

1" PIPE
THROUGHOUT

4x6 s

ROPE

PORTABLE
DECK

2x4 s

WALKING
BOARD

4x4 BALANCE
BEAM

ALL POSTS 4x4

SAWHORSE
(SEE FIG. 16)

JUNIOR OLYMPIAN

FOUNDATIONS (TYPICAL)
SEE FIG. 25

Figure 30

84

JUNIOR OLYMPIAN

The Junior Olympian design focuses on the development of physical skills. The horizontal ladder can be fitted with hand rings and a trapeze bar. Cut the hand rings from one-inch wood and attach them with rope; make the trapeze bar from a one-inch hardwood dowel. Connect these attachments with an S-hook to an eye bolt at the support ladder so they can be quickly removed and not interfere with active use of the horizontal ladder.

You can adjust the height of the turning bar and the parallel bars. If this unit will be used by both children and adults, it would be a good idea to add another chinning bar at a different height. This can be attached either to the outside support of the existing bar or to the opposite side of the structure.

As shown in Figure 30, the back section of the structure acts as an adjustable support for balance beams and inclined boards. The portable decks allow this section to be used for creative play when it is not being used for motor development.

The construction materials specified here have been selected for maximum strength and durability. Use large wooden sections and galvanized pipe instead of wooden doweling. A structure of the same configuration, built using the ladder system shown in the previous design, would be appropriate if it will be used by small children only. The assumption in the design as illustrated is that both adults and children will use the structure. If lightweight materials are selected, the unit should be constructed to a seven-eighths scale. Do this by multiplying the dimensions given on the plan by the factor of .875.

Under View of Movable Deck

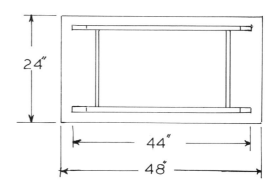

Edge View of Movable Deck

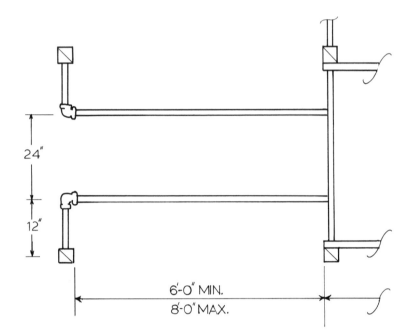

JUNIOR OLYMPIAN

Plan View

24"

12"

6'-0" MIN.
8'-0" MAX.

Side View

6"

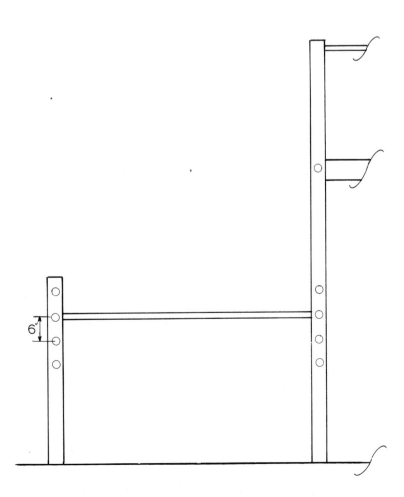

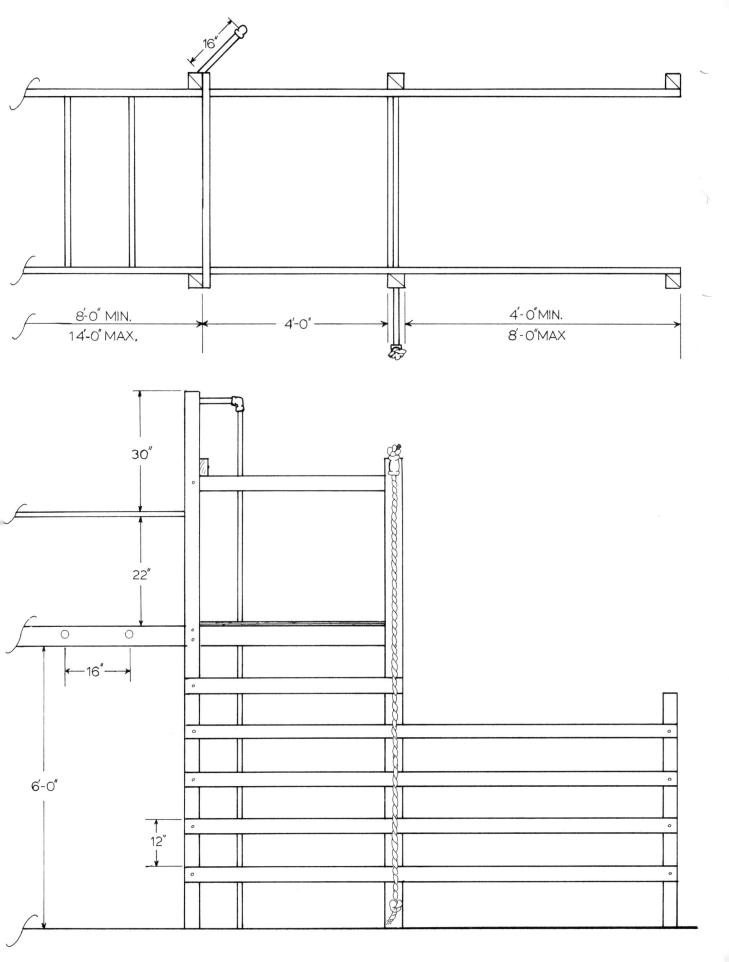

16"

8'-0" MIN.
14'-0" MAX.

4'-0"

4'-0"MIN.
8'-0"MAX

30"

22"

16"

6'-0"

12"

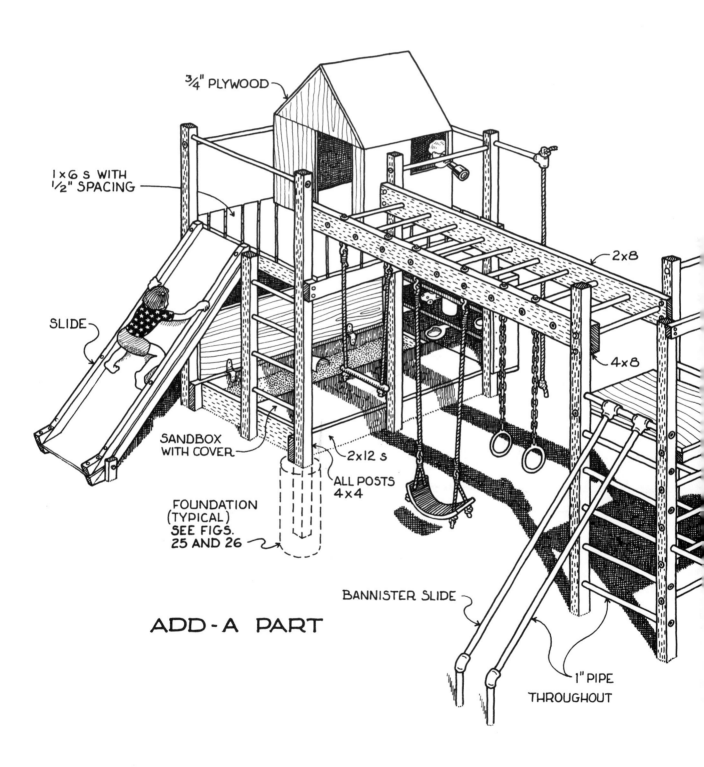

¾" PLYWOOD

1x6 s WITH ½" SPACING

SLIDE

SANDBOX WITH COVER

FOUNDATION (TYPICAL) SEE FIGS. 25 AND 26

2x12 s

ALL POSTS 4x4

2x8

4x8

BANNISTER SLIDE

1" PIPE THROUGHOUT

ADD-A PART

88

ADD-A-PART

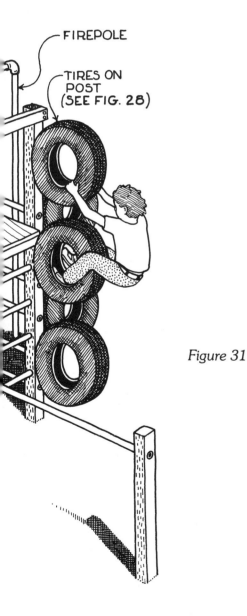

FIREPOLE

TIRES ON POST (SEE FIG. 28)

Figure 31

If you don't need portability and can't build in a tree, then the Add-a-Part design may be the best for you. Unlike the Clubhouse, which is intended for young children, this design serves all ages. It is, however, a very large structure and might be best constructed in phases. It has four distinct parts which can be built separately, and each will function well as an independent unit.

The sandbox is designed with a lid to keep out cats and a roof to provide shade. The roof is also a platform from which a slide exits. A small playhouse could be placed on the roof of the sandbox or it could be left at ground level.

The swing and horizontal ladder component could be built independently or it could be added on to the sandbox if that structure is built first. The tower section could be added at a later date, as part of the swing component, or it could be the first stage. Thus, this design makes it possible to construct those parts which meet your immediate needs and resources.

Notice that the sandbox is not only covered, it also has built-in storage. When the sand is uncovered, the lid forms a low side so the only entry is under the slide. The net effect of this design is to create a very cozy sand play area that is well sheltered from the more active play around it.

The playhouse is the simplest of boxes.

ADD-A-PART

Removable Clubhouse
End View

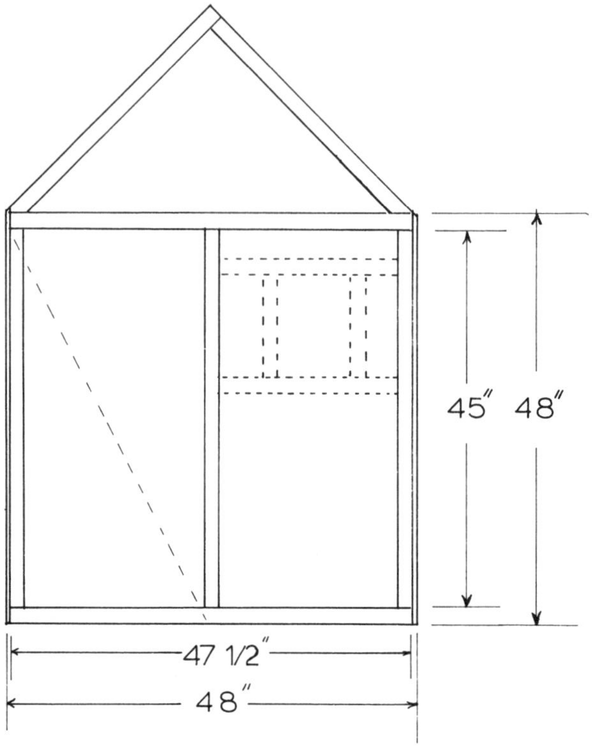

Normally, such a plain design would not be successful as a play component; here it works well because it is only a small part of a complex environment. Part of its success stems from the porch area around the outside of the house. This creates an inside/outside contrast that contributes to the overall play dynamics. Being off the ground also enhances the effect.

The three-station swing frame allows for a wide variety of components, including a tire swing. Attaching them with two S-hooks will allow quick adaptability for different age groups.

The tower not only provides for a number of important motor skills, it also functions as a separate island during dramatic play. This effect could be heightened by putting a steering wheel at both the main and tower decks. The deck itself could be made detachable so that it can be either removed entirely or adjusted for height. The tire climber area can be made more complex by adding a free-standing tire tree, as shown in the Clubhouse design.

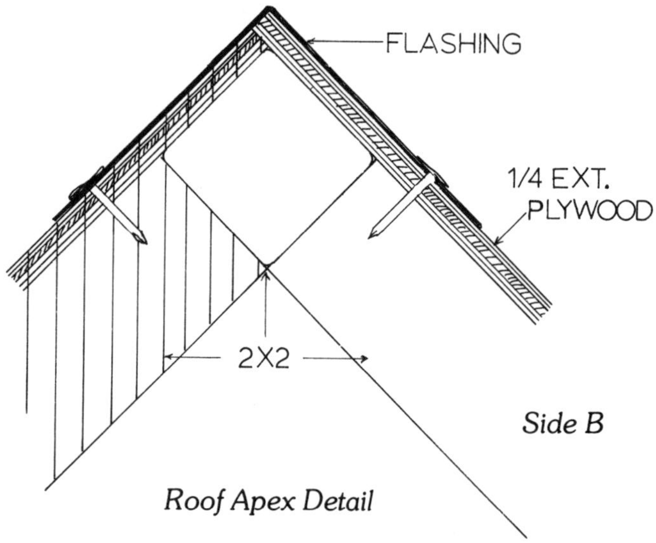

45″ 48″

47 1/2″

48″

FLASHING

1/4 EXT. PLYWOOD

Side A

2X2

Side B

Roof Apex Detail

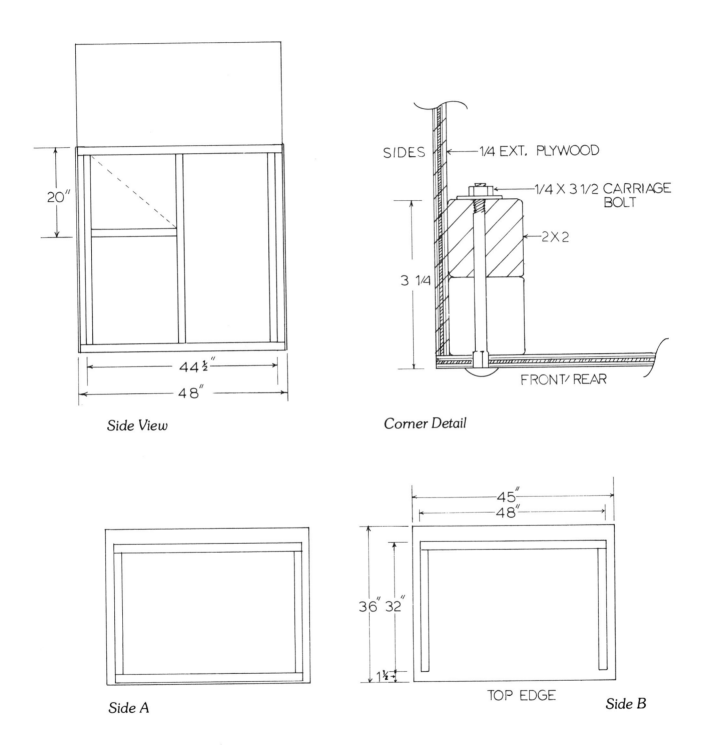

Side View

SIDES

1/4 EXT. PLYWOOD

1/4 X 3 1/2 CARRIAGE BOLT

2 X 2

3 1/4

FRONT/ REAR

Corner Detail

20"

44 ½"

48"

45"

48"

36" 32"

1½"

TOP EDGE

Side A

Side B

Roof Details of Removable Clubhouse

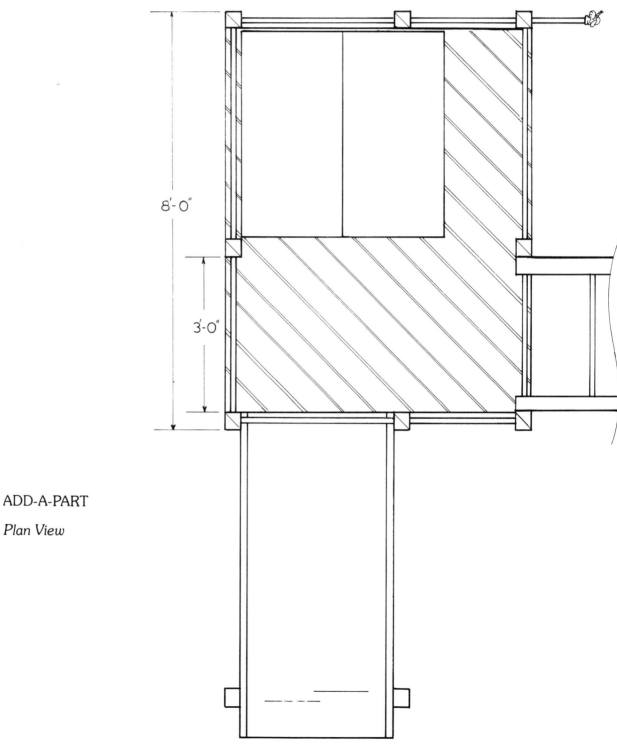

ADD-A-PART

Plan View

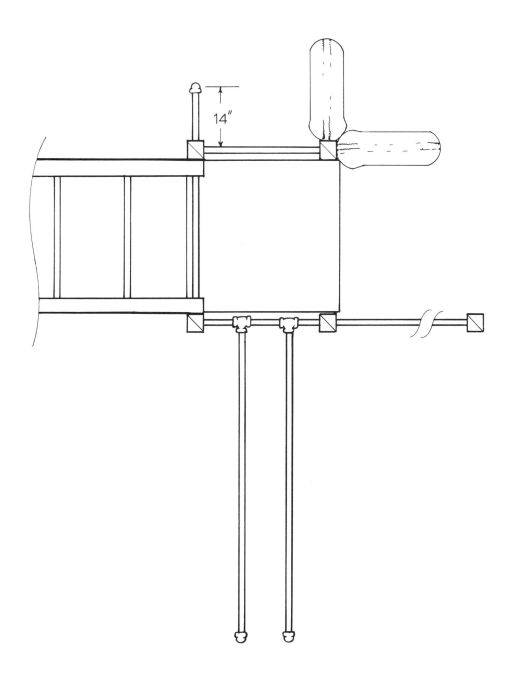

14"

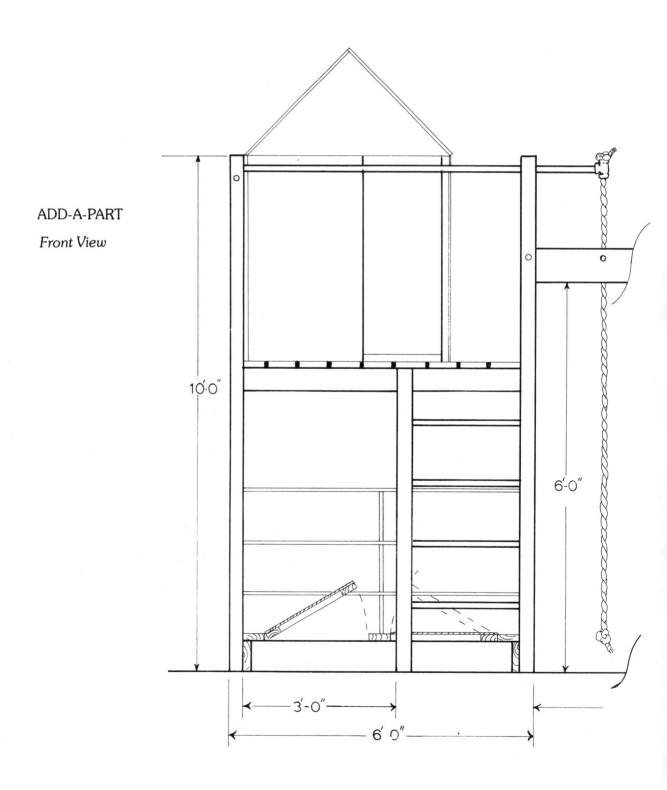

ADD-A-PART

Front View

10'-0"

6'-0"

3'-0"

6' 0"

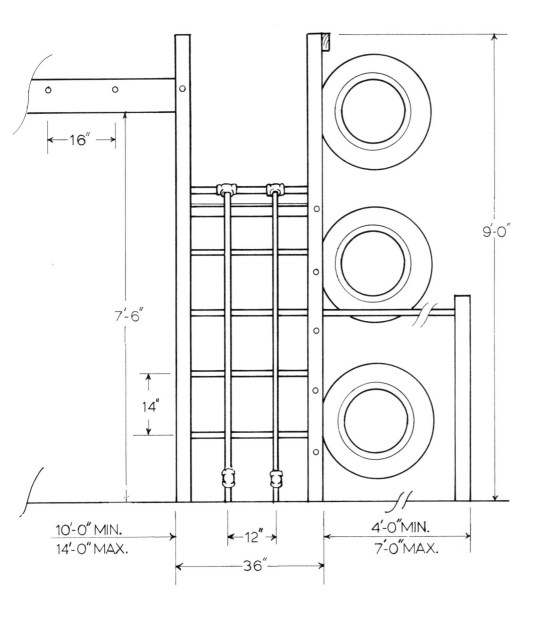

16"

7'-6"

14"

9'-0"

10'-0" MIN.
14'-0" MAX.

12"

4'-0" MIN.
7'-0" MAX.

36"

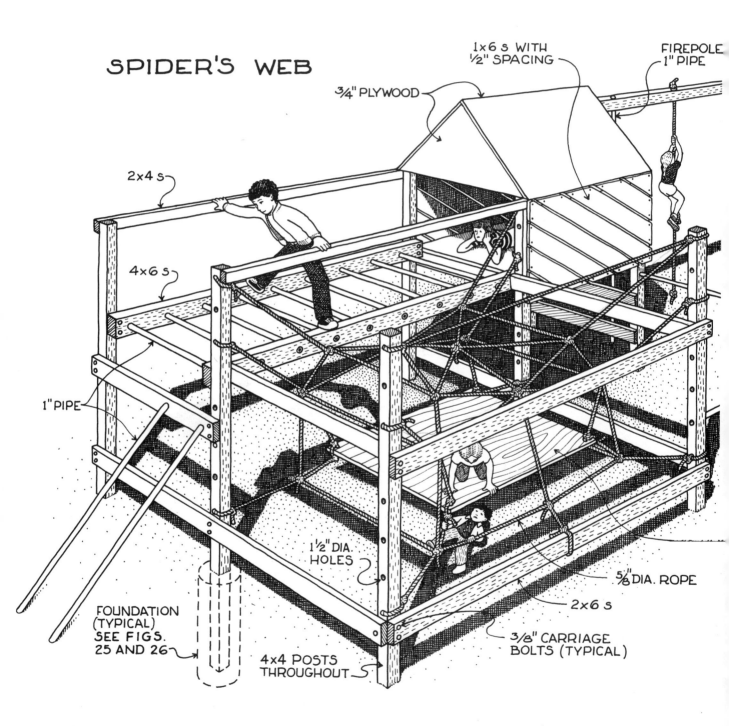

SPIDER'S WEB

1x6 s WITH ½" SPACING

FIREPOLE 1" PIPE

¾" PLYWOOD

2x4 s

4x6 s

1" PIPE

1½" DIA. HOLES

FOUNDATION (TYPICAL) SEE FIGS. 25 AND 26

4x4 POSTS THROUGHOUT

5⁄8" DIA. ROPE

2x6 s

3⁄8" CARRIAGE BOLTS (TYPICAL)

SPIDER'S WEB

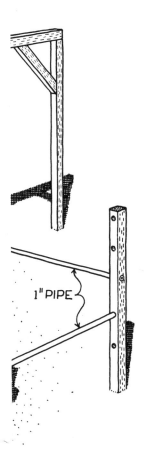

1" PIPE

- ¾" PLYWOOD
PLATFORM

Figure 32

This is an interesting design because it can grow with your children and also provides for a lot of play in a very small space. The horizontal ladder first supports tot swings and then standard swings. Later, when the second-story clubhouse is added, a higher support frame can be built for more challenging swing activities. In this design, the turning bars are fully adjustable and can be moved progressively higher.

The area below the deck of the clubhouse is too small to be developed into the kind of sand play area that was featured in the Add-a-Part design, but it can still be an interesting place to play. A steering wheel or canvas sides will do a lot for its appeal.

What really sets this design apart from any other is the Spider's Web. This feature is unbelievably appealing to children. It draws them like a magnet and keeps them entertained for hours.

The design is nothing more than a platform suspended by ropes, but the slight movement seems to evoke great fantasies of ships and rockets. The rope network demands a lot of climbing skill, and yet even fairly young children can use it, if supervised.

This rope environment is so successful at stimulating fantasy play that it could function very well without any other equipment. Spider Webs can also be added to some of the other designs presented in this book.

Since all it requires are four strong corners, rope, and a small piece of plywood, there is no reason that it could not be a feature of most play areas.

There is nothing magic about the construction of the Spider's Web. The ropes simply pass through holes drilled into the support framework and are joined by square knots. The deck itself is just a piece of plywood with four one-inch holes at the corners. The plywood could be replaced with a tire, or even two tires at different heights.

Remember two points when putting the ropes in place. First, rope stretches quite a bit and you should provide for some convenient method of adjusting the slack so that you won't have to take apart knots that have been under a considerable load. The best place to make these adjustments is at the top of each support post. The second rope down from the top can also help tighten up the web, or you can add more rope connections at various points to make adjustments.

Second, rope does wear and you will have to inspect the web regularly. Pay particular attention to the upper joints, where the rope attaches to the frame, and to the connections of the rope and the plywood deck.

A word of caution also seems appropriate. While the Spider's Web is a very low-hazard structure, one feature might present a problem. Make sure the openings in the net are large enough so a basketball could pass through them, even when there is weight in the net. If you use this standard, there is very little chance of creating an area which might entrap a child.

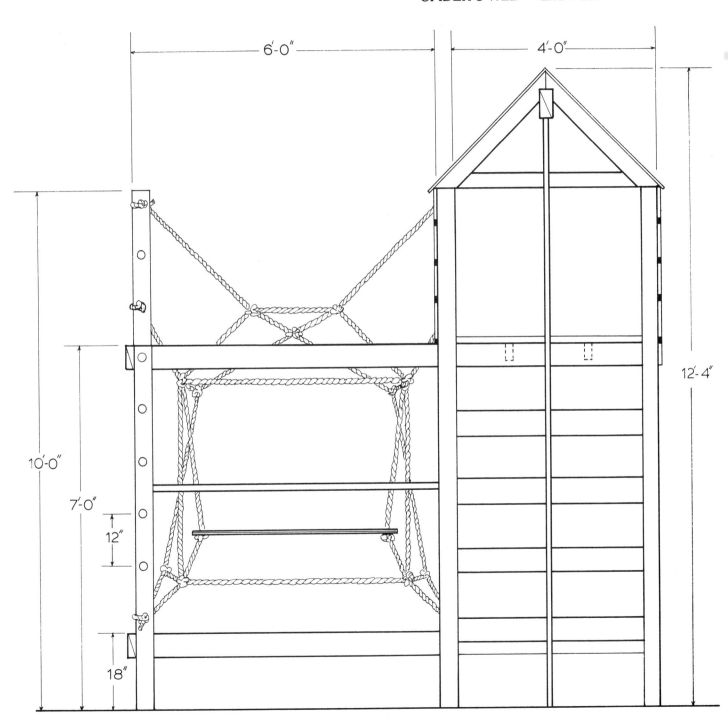

SPIDER'S WEB   *End View*

6'-0"

4'-0"

12'-4"

10'-0"

7'-0"

12"

18"

SPIDER'S WEB *Plan View*

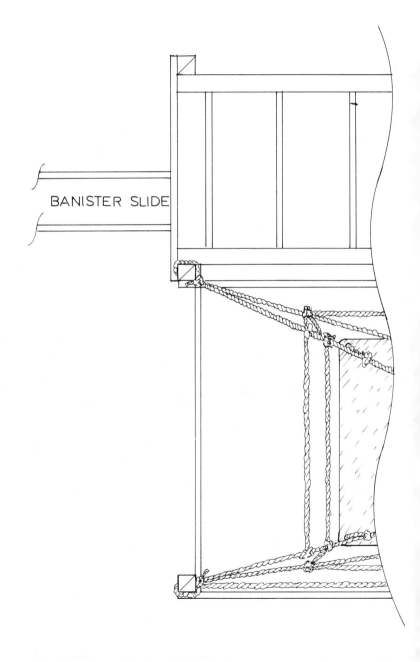

BANISTER SLIDE

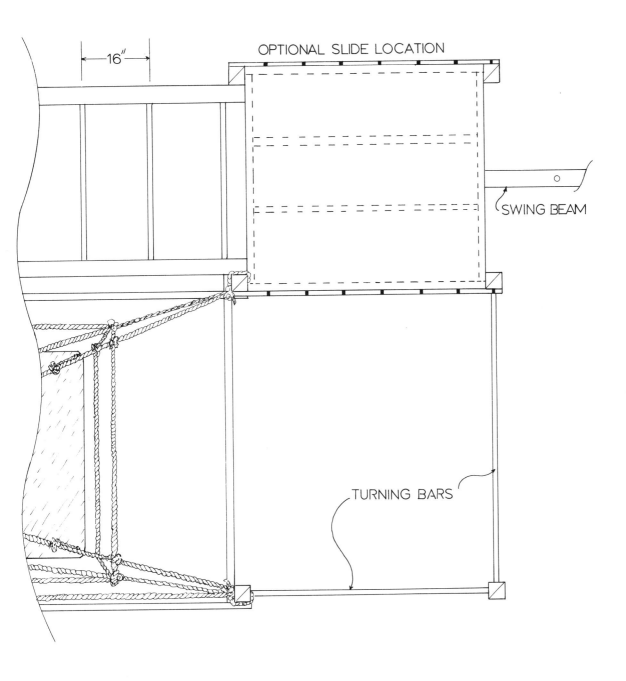

OPTIONAL SLIDE LOCATION

16"

SWING BEAM

TURNING BARS

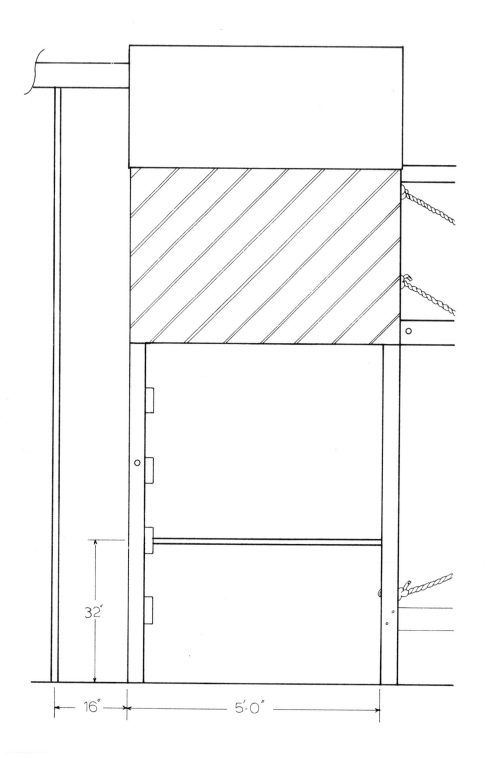

32"

16"

5'-0"

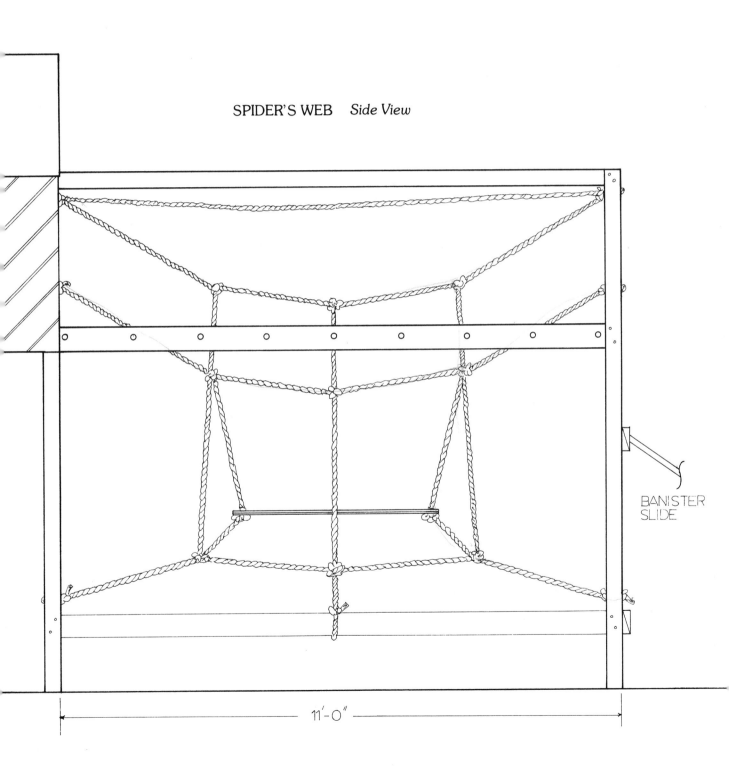

SPIDER'S WEB   *Side View*

BANISTER
SLIDE

11'-0"

MODULAR COMPONENTS

Don't let the size of this design scare you. Most of the designs shown in this book could be expanded into an equally complex environment. What we have done here is to reproduce a few simple components many times and put them into various configurations.

The back half is nothing more than a mirror image of the front half, and the front half is two nearly identical parts with the decks at different levels. The decks themselves are all alike as are the side panels located at two different levels. These modular components make this design very easy to build.

One of the best features of this design is that it does not require footed posts. Like the Portable Climber shown earlier, it can be disassembled very easily. Instead of a maze of ladders, this unit can be made very colorful. Another advantage of this design is the use of larger materials which makes it inherently more stable.

Plywood and 4 x 4s are the main components of this system. You can build it inexpensively with "merchandisable" grade 4 x 4s and "exterior shop" grade plywood. Or, you could spend three times as much on materials and buy redwood posts and "medium density overlay" plywood.

The illustration shows four modules with a horizontal ladder, rope bridges, tire walk, and tunnel connecting the front and back halves. Two modules can be placed about

eight feet apart, with a rope or tire bridge connecting the upper portions and a tunnel connecting the lower decks. You can attach a horizontal ladder and swing frame to this two-module unit, making it nearly as complex as the structure shown, but involving substantially less building.

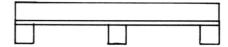

Front Edge View of Deck

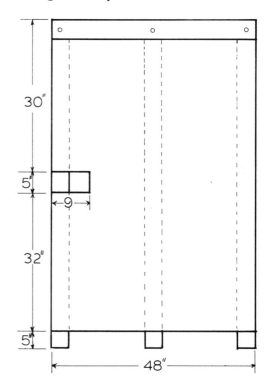

Plan View Detail of Deck

MODULAR COMPONENTS *Plan View*

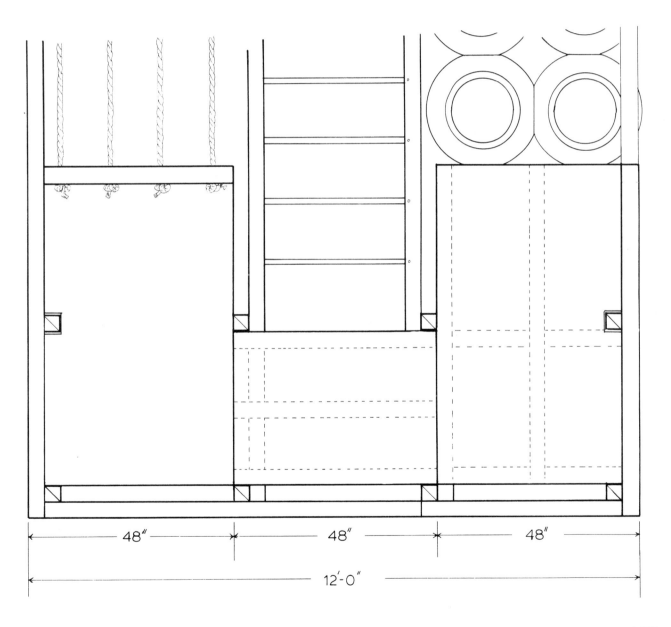

48″ 48″ 48″

12′-0″

Figure 33

MODULAR COMPONENTS   *Front View of Side Panel*

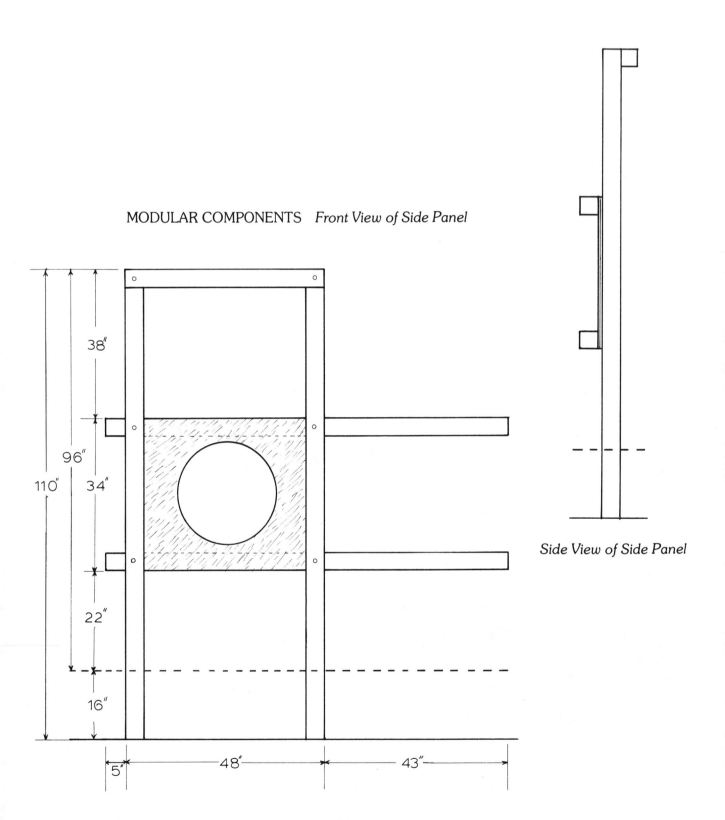

Side View of Side Panel

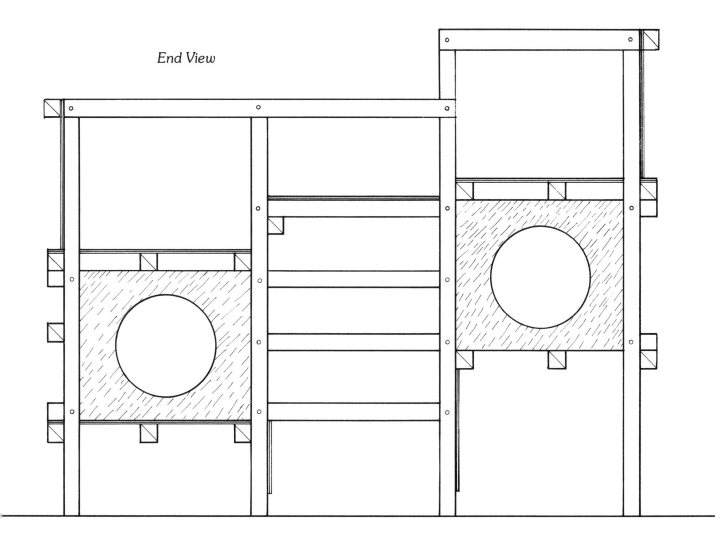

End View

ADVENTURE PLAY AREA

The Adventure Play Area is an extension of the sandbox with loose parts. What have been added here are larger components like big cable spools and wooden crates. The kids should be old enough to use a hammer and nails to get the most out of this sort of play area.

The crates and spools will form the basis of the constructions, and will need to be reinforced. A shipping box loses much of its strength when the top is taken off. Plywood corner braces or 1 x 4 diagonal braces will give the box the needed rigidity.

Cable spools invariably need to be tightened. Do this by tightening the through bolts at the top and bottom of the spool. Every spring, when the wood starts to dry out, you will have to do this again. Paint the spools and crates to keep them from absorbing too much water and they will last longer.

In addition to spools and crates, gather ladders, old doors, various lengths of wood, large pieces of canvas, and other construction materials. When kids combine them with a couple of hammers and nails, the Adventure Play Area happens by itself. (Or, almost by itself, since there are some things parents still have to monitor.)

Stepping on nails seems to be the most frequent mishap in this kind of play area, so kids must wear hard-soled shoes. This may be difficult in the era of sneakers, but you must make every effort to enforce the rule.

Parents must also check the kids' con-structions for structural strength. The "wiggle test" works as well as any. This involves climbing onto the structure and wiggling it. If it moves a great deal and is obviously weak, you should ask the kids to reinforce it, or add a few crossbars and extra nails yourself. It is wise to set a height limit and to require that none of the structures be taller than the child, or higher than he can reach from the ground.

Besides monitoring the Adventure Play Area for structural integrity and general safety, it is a good idea to check the supply of materials periodically. Nails are used up at an incredible rate, and lumber is always in short supply. New materials and ideas are always welcomed.

A trip to the army surplus store, Salvation Army Thrift Store, construction sites, and even junk yards will maintain the kids' interest in the Adventure Play Area. (The trip to the junk yard will not be necessarily to gather new material, but to dump old stuff.) Just buying several quarts of paint in various colors will bring a high level of excitement to the area.

Like the Treehouse, the Adventure Play Area has somewhat more risk involved than the other, more structured environments. Therefore, it is especially important to follow the safety suggestions described earlier so that parents of visiting children are made aware of the activities their children will be enjoying when they play in your backyard.

ADVENTURE PLAY AREA

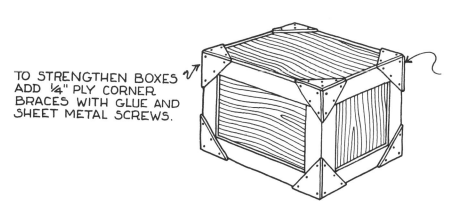

TO STRENGTHEN BOXES
ADD ¼" PLY CORNER
BRACES WITH GLUE AND
SHEET METAL SCREWS.

Figure 34

ANNOTATED BIBLIOGRAPHY

Activities

Caney, Steven. *Play Book & Toy Book.* New York: Workman Publishing Company, 1975 & 1972, paperback.

Steve has collected more neat things to do than any other person. There are games and toys that you forgot years ago, and many that will be completely new to you as well. Written so most third graders could follow the instructions.

Cardoza, Peter. *The Whole Kids Catalog & The Second Whole Kids Catalog.* New York: Bantam Books, Inc., 1975 & 1977, paperback.

Source and resource books of even more complexity than the Play and Toy books above. Targeted for kids from the fifth grade up, these books make a perfect extension of the kinds of activities begun earlier in Steve's works.

Cherry, Clare. *Creative Play for the Developing Child: Early Lifehood Education Through Play.* Belmont, Calif.: Fearon Publishers, Inc., 1976, paperback.

This book was written for nursery school teachers, but is an excellent source of information for parents. If you intend to actively facilitate the play activities of your children, this book will give you solid techniques.

Dean, Joan. *Room to Learn.* New York: Citation Press, 1972, paperback.

Another book intended for teachers, but full of good ideas for parents. Particularly valuable for its detailed information on storage. Tells how to use common or recycled materials to create exceptional play/learning areas. Recently reprinted in three separate small booklets: *Working Space, A Place to Paint,* and *Language Areas* for $1.95 each.

Ferretti, Fred. *The Great American Book of Sidewalk, Stoop, Dirt, Curb, and Alley Games.* New York: Workman Publishing Company, 1975, paperback.

Written by a guy who's only grown up on the outside, this book contains all the classic street games played in America. Easy-to-understand instructions.

Fluegelman, Andrew (ed). *The New Games Book.* New York: Dolphin Books/Doubleday & Company, Inc., paperback.

Many of these games aren't really new; they've been played for eons by Eskimos and Bantus. What is new is that these are games in which everybody is a winner. You can teach them to your kids and they will often play them of their own initiative. Indispensable for parties, whether it's kids who don't know what to do with themselves or grownups who think having a good time can only involve putting food and drink in their mouths.

Milberg, Alan. *Street Games*. New York: McGraw-Hill Book Company, 1976, paperback.

Even more activities than Ferretti's book—describes and gives instruction for an incredible number of games.

Singer, Dorothy G. and Jerome L. *Partners in Play: A Step-by-Step Guide to Imaginative Play in Childhood*. New York: Harper and Row, 1977.

Written by the foremost child development psychologists in America, this lovingly crafted book gives practical ideas and methods for parents' interactions with their children that open up the creative potential which may have been dampened by TV or poor schools. The Singers have a deep understanding of the role of fantasy in the developing intelligence of the child, and they communicate their wisdom in a manner that every parent can appreciate.

Play

Bruner, Jerome S., et al. (eds). *Play—Its Role in Development and Evolution*. New York: Basic Books, Inc., 1976.

This is *the* book on play. It brings together most of the important literature and research in the field. Intended primarily for professionals and academicians, it is fascinating reading for parents.

Caplan, Frank and Theresa. *The Power of Play*. New York: Anchor Press/Doubleday , 1974, paperback.

This very large book tells you everything important about play and its role in child development. Intended for educators and parents alike.

DeKoven, Bernard. *The Well-Played Game: A Player's Philosophy*. New York: Anchor Press/Doubleday , 1978, paperback.

DeKoven helped start New Games and it touched his life. Since then he has set up the Game Preserve in Fleetwood, Pennsylvania where he continues to study and play with others to try to discover what exactly it is that he has gotten in touch with through play. *The Well-Played Game* admits you to the mystical adventure he is making.

Herron, R. E. and Sutton-Smith, Brian (ed). *Child's Play*. New York: John Wiley & Sons, Inc., 1971.

A book of readings in the anthropology and psychology of play for professionals.

Levy, Joseph. *Play Behavior*. New York: John Wiley & Sons, Inc., 1978.

A small book, but very carefully done so that all of the major theories of play are covered in a clear and concise manner.

Play as Therapy

Reed, Jeannette Pruyn. *Sand Magic, Experience in Miniature: A Non-Verbal Therapy for Children*. Albuquerque: JPR Publishers, paperback.

This privately published book by the author details her extensive experience using a simple sandbox and a collection of miniature toys to communicate on a very profound level with children.

Moustakas, Clark E. *Children in Play Therapy*. New York: Ballantine Books, 1974, paperback.

For everyone who would really like to learn how to listen to children and develop the patience to be a good parent, this book is essential.

Sensorimotor Activities for the Remediation of Learning Disabilities. San Rafael, California: Academic Therapy Publications.

A book that was written as a collaborative effort with teachers and therapists with assistance from a federal grant. This work details corrective activities and explains the underlying physical conditions for many learning problems.

Wolfgang, Charles H. *Helping Aggressive and Passive Preschoolers Through Play*. Columbus, Ohio: Charles E. Merrill Publishing Company, 1977.

A simple and easily used technique for helping kids modify behaviors which are socially unproductive.

TV and the Whole Child

Brown, Ray (ed). *Children and Television*. Beverly Hills: Sage Publications, Inc., 1976, paperback.

Readings in the relationship between TV and kids from the sociologist's point of view.

Coppola, Raymond T. *Successful Children*. New York: Walker and Company, 1978.

We'd all like to have kids who are geniuses. Since that's not possible, at least we'd like to have kids who feel (and are in fact) successful. While there are limits to what parents can do, this book suggests many practical approaches that parents will find surprisingly effective. There is a particularly good chapter on turning TV into a learning tool.

Mander, Jerry. *Four Arguments for the Elimination of Television*. New York: William Morrow and Company, Inc., 1978, paperback.

A well thought out and accurate critique of TV. After reading this book you will know why TV is awful, instead of having only vague suspicions.

Pearce, Joseph Chilton. *Magical Child: Rediscovering Nature's Plan for Our Children*. New York: E. P. Dutton, 1977.

Not a book about TV, but about whole children and what they can become. The ideas in the book seemed to some a little left of the radical fringe when it first appeared, but many of Pearce's insights have since been validated by research.

Winn, Marie. *The Plug-In Drug.* New York: Bantam Books, 1977, paperback.

    Readable and complete. Not only tells you why TV is bad, but that it is possible to kick the habit.

Physical Education

Anderson, Marian H., et al. (eds.). *Play with a Purpose: Elementary School Physical Education.* New York: Harper and Row, 1972, paperback.

    The complete elementary school physical education curricula.

Bentley, William G. *Learning to Move and Moving to Learn.* New York: Citation Press, 1970, paperback.

    A small book, but loaded with movement education activities. Well illustrated.

Flinchum, Betty M., Ph.D. *Motor Development in Early Childhood: A Guide for Movement Education with Ages Two to Six.* St. Louis: The C. V. Mosby Company, 1975.

    More comprehensive than Bentley's book and aimed at slightly younger children.

Kirchner, Glenn, et al. *Introduction to Movement Education: An Individualized Approach to Teaching Physical Education.* Dubuque, Iowa: Wm. C. Brown Company, 1977, paperback.

    This approach is unique. Instead of setting up specific tasks, the method here is to give assignments which can be creatively solved by the children. In this way there is no right or wrong response.

Safety

Green, Martin I. (producer). *A Sigh of Relief: The First-Aid Handbook for Childhood Emergencies.* New York: Bantam Books, 1977, paperback.

    Indexed for fast reference, with instructions that can be read in a few seconds, and incorporates the most up-to-date procedures. This book really does what it sets out to do: provide accurate and instant first-aid information. No home with children should be without it.

Play Happy, Play Safely. Produced by the Consumer Product Safety Commission. Office of the Secretary, 5401 Westbard Avenue, Bethesda, Maryland 20207.

MATERIALS

BigToys
3113 South Pine Street
Tacoma, Washington 98409
206/572-7611
    Manufacturers of high-quality log and pipe structures for homes, parks, and schools.
    Mail order and national sales representatives. Custom designs possible.

Childcraft Education Corporation
20 Kilmer Road
Edison, New Jersey 08817
800/631-5652
    Catalog sales of educational toys and games. Regional sales representatives.

Child Life Play Specialties, Inc.
55 Whitney Street
Holliston, Massachusetts 01746
617/429-4639
    Manufacturers of ladder-type play structures for homes. Cable ride, swing hardware, and other attachments also available separately.
    Mail order and quality toy stores.

F. A. O. Schwarz
5th Avenue at 58th Street
New York, New York 10022
    Catalog 50 cents for wide range of toys.

Catalog

If you are interested in a list of fine Paperback
books, covering a wide range of subjects
and interests, send your name and address,
requesting your free catalog, to:

McGraw-Hill Paperbacks
1221 Avenue of Americas
New York, N.Y. 10020